The **Mis**adventures of Marvin

*With Warmest
Best Wishes*

Marvin Dwyer

The
Misadventures
of Marvin

Marvin Druger

Syracuse University Press

Copyright © 2010 by Syracuse University Press
Syracuse, New York, 13244-5290

All Rights Reserved

First Edition 2010

10 11 12 13 14 15   6 5 4 3 2 1

Marvin Druger's poem "The Grump" is from *Strange Creatures and Other Poems*,
Druger by the Lake Publisher, 2004.

∞ The paper used in this publication meets the minimum requirements
of the American National Standard for Information Sciences—Permanence
of Paper for Printed Library Materials, ANSI Z39.48-1992.

For a listing of books published and distributed by Syracuse University Press,
visit our Web site at SyracuseUniversityPress.syr.edu.

ISBN: 978-0-8156-0949-0

Library of Congress Cataloging-in-Publication Data

Druger, Marvin.
    The misadventures of Marvin / Marvin Druger. — 1st ed.
        p. cm.
    ISBN 978-0-8156-0949-0 (pbk. : alk. paper)
    1. Druger, Marvin—Anecdotes.   2. College teachers—New York (State)—
Biography—Anecdotes.   3. Interpersonal relations—Anecdotes.   4. Conduct
of life.   I. Title.
    CT275.D8756A3 2010
    974.7'043092—dc22
    [B]   2009052610

Manufactured in the United States of America

Contents

Illustrations

Illustrations

Preface

This book is about life and relationships. Much of what happens to an individual in a lifetime is generalizable. We see much of ourselves in the misadventures of others, and we can laugh about these incidents. Marvin has lived more than seventy-five years, and has been married to the same woman for more than fifty-two years. They have three grown children and seven grandchildren of varying ages. This book will reveal many awkward and laughable moments in Marvin's life. Real names are not used to protect the innocent. All of the incidents are true, but some may have become a bit exaggerated in memory. When Marvin told a friend that this book describes all the stupid things that he has done in his life, his wife commented, "And it's a very fat book."

1. Pat and Marvin. Photo by Steve Sartori.

Acknowledgments

This book represents more than seventy-five years of interacting with people. Every person I met in life had a part in developing this book and I am grateful to everyone for providing the many experiences that I can share with readers. I sincerely appreciate the love, patience, and support of my wife, Pat. Tolerating me for more than fifty-two years of marriage should merit sainthood for her. Our children (Lauren, Robert, and James) and our grandchildren (Keith, Lindsey, Aaron, Joshua, Rachel, Gabrielle, and Teagan) offered encouragement and love that are much appreciated. Thanks to Steve Sartori, manager of the Photo and Imaging Center at Syracuse University, for taking photos of Pat and me whenever he saw us and for providing many of the photos in this book. Thanks to Kathleen Pollard for her technical assistance. I also appreciate the enthusiastic encouragement and support of Mary Selden Evans, executive editor of the Syracuse University Press. I could name many others who have been helpful and supportive, but the list would be almost endless. So, thanks to all.

The **Mis**adventures of Marvin

1 Love and Marriage

How I Met the Love of My Life

I was president, vice president, social secretary, and treasurer of Lyons House Plan at Brooklyn College, all at the same time. A house plan was similar to a fraternity, but the members lived at home. I arranged three parties for Easter week. Two were with college sororities and the other was with a high school sorority. I told my friends that I wasn't going to the high school party (I was twenty years old and those girls were too young for me). "If you don't go, then we're not going" was the response . . . so I went. I saw this cute girl there with short, dark hair and a pretty face. I tried to have a conversation with her, but she didn't seem attracted to me (I had pimples). Instead, she seemed to prefer Arnold, a tall, handsome friend of mine. I edged him out and talked to Pat.

She was a smoker, and she said, "I wish I had a cigarette."

"C'mon," I replied, "Let's walk to the candy store and I'll buy you a pack."

"A whole pack?" she said with surprise. Since then, I claimed that I bought her first whole pack of cigarettes. (Years later, she told me that she did make that remark, but she thought that I looked too cheap to buy her a whole pack of cigarettes.)

Finally, I asked her if I could walk her home to her family's apartment on East Fourteenth Street. She said yes, and I walked with her toward her home. She asked, "Do you know how old I am?"

"You must be seventeen or eighteen," I replied.

"I'm fifteen," she said. I was so shocked that we walked around the block once more. (Baby stuff . . . robbing the cradle. . . . She was much too young for a twenty-year-old college man like me.) We rode the elevator to the fifth floor. I walked with her down the hallway to her apartment, about twenty-five feet away from the elevator. (Nice girl, but she was much too young for me.)

I said goodnight and walked back to the elevator. For some reason, she fumbled with her keys and couldn't find the right one. For some reason, the elevator was on another floor. It was less than ten seconds later when I thought, "Gee, I kind of liked her." I walked back and said, "Pat, if I don't ask you out now, I'll probably never see you again. Do you want to go to a movie with me next Friday?" (I had another date for Saturday night.) "Okay," she replied, unenthusiastically.

The next Friday, we went to the Fox theater in downtown Brooklyn. In the movie theater, she put her arm around me. (Hey . . . that was nice . . . I really liked her.) One thing led to another, and we were eventually married. Since then, we managed to have three children, seven grandchildren, two cars, four houses (including a lake house with two kayaks, a motorboat, a sailboat, paddleboats, a rowboat, and a variety of water accessories), and a happy life together.

I often think about the night we met. Suppose Pat had immediately found the right key to her apartment, and suppose the elevator had been there on the fifth floor. I didn't know her last name, I didn't have her phone number, and I lived in a different neighborhood. I would probably never have seen her again, and life would have turned out quite differently for both of us.

This was a lesson to point out to my students. Life can easily be changed by a single event, and that's why it's so important to attend classes and have as many different experiences as possible. The more experiences you have, the more likely it is that some critical event may occur that will change your entire life. You never know.

Girlfriends

Meeting fifteen-year-old Pat was a milestone in my life. We dated and my life started to change. I had a real girlfriend. I had had other girlfriends before Pat, but nothing serious. Renee dumped me for someone else. I was devastated. Iris's family owned something new called a "television set." It was a huge box with a tiny screen. We enjoyed holding hands and watching the *Milton Berle Show* and the *Ed Sullivan Show* in black-and-white. The men of Texaco looked very small. Then Iris and I drifted apart.

3

My girlfriends had sofas and rugs in their apartments. My apartment had linoleum on the floor and stiff wooden chairs. My friends were also poor, but I think I was the poorest. Or maybe not—one friend told me that he was so poor that he had to share a winter coat with his brother, so that he and his brother couldn't go out of their apartment at the same time in the winter.

Pat and I were together for awhile, and we were "going steady." Then Pat had second thoughts and wanted to go out on a date with someone else. I decided that, if she could date someone else, so could I. Her date fell through. I went out on a date with some other girl and spent the entire evening telling her about Pat. After that evening, we stayed faithfully with each other.

After dating for two years, Pat and I decided to get engaged. By that time, I was a graduate student in the zoology department at Columbia University. In those days, girls were engaged at age sixteen and they had to have a large diamond ring. I tutored the daughter of a rich executive and earned enough money to buy Pat a one-and-a-quarter carat diamond ring. Her parents didn't like the fact that we decided to become engaged. Pat's parents were rich, compared to my parents. They had visions of their only daughter marrying a rich doctor or lawyer, and they didn't want to mix with poor in-laws. The age difference did not seem important. Despite the reluctance of her parents, we got engaged, and, six months later, we decided to get married. Her parents objected, but when they saw that we were about to elope, they decided to finance a wedding for us. I was the

2. Pat and Marvin at their wedding on June 9, 1957. Photo by
Charles Sanders.

first among my childhood friends to get married, and all
my friends attended the wedding. The supper club owner
invited us to a free dinner a week after the wedding, since
he felt that we were both too nervous to enjoy the food on

5

our wedding day. Eating a good meal and getting married didn't seem to go well together. Pat and I were about to begin more than fifty-two years of adventures together.

How to Stay Married for Fifty Years or More

June 9, 2009, marked our fifty-second wedding anniversary. That's a long time to remain with one spouse, especially nowadays when divorces are so common. What are the secrets for such a long marriage? From my perspective, there are some simple guidelines:

Compromise. Do everything she says and don't ask questions. "Yes, dear" goes a long way in a marriage.

Let her handle the money. I don't do money in the household. Pat handles all financial matters. I only have a vague idea of my annual income. My salary has always been a mystery to me. So, Pat can buy whatever she wants, and I'll never know about it, or care.

I get an allowance. My allowance is $100 per week, payable on the fifteenth of each month in a lump sum of $400. This allowance is for lunches, gasoline, and miscellaneous expenses. I have very few needs, so I put most of the money in a small coffee can that I have hidden in a closet in the house. I hide this money in case I need funds for a sudden expense, like taking a weekend trip to Hawaii. It is satisfying to know that I have *my* own money that is not *her* money. Usually, what's hers is hers, and what's mine is hers!

After many years of stashing away the leftovers from my allowance, I finally decided that I would deposit the coffee-can money in a savings bank. I was surprised and pleased to discover that I had accumulated $7,000. Wow!

I also fold a few $100 dollar bills into secret pockets in my wallet, and use the money to buy Pat gifts. When I see something that I think she would like, I buy it.

I saw a pair of very nice earrings in a store. I bought them for her. A few months later, while in that same store, I saw another pair of earrings that I thought she would like. I bought them for her. A few months later, I saw yet another pair of earrings in that store that I thought she'd like, and I bought them.

It turned out that I bought exactly the same earrings three different times. My daughter now has one pair, my granddaughter has one pair, and Pat kept the other pair. I guess I have a poor memory about earrings.

When the price of gasoline soared, I asked Pat for a raise in allowance. That month, she gave me $50 more than usual. The next month, she forgot about the raise. I reminded her. Big mistake. She became very angry and said, "From now on, you handle the finances. I don't want to have anything to do with it." So, as you might guess, I was back to $400 per month. However, I made an interesting discovery. I can slide a card into a slot on the gas pump and, since Pat handles all the bills, I get the gas for free.

Do things together. We manage to spend a lot of time together, yet we maintain our individuality. We are best friends, yet we watch different TV programs in different rooms. Mutual respect for different interests yet sharing friendship and love are key elements to a successful marriage.

I make the big decisions and she makes the other decisions. I decide if we will invade some alien country, or if we will drop an atomic bomb somewhere, or if we will raise taxes. Pat makes all the other decisions. I have a sign hanging on the wall in my home office. It says, "If at first you don't succeed, try doing it the way your wife told you."

When I told these golden rules to others, Pat claimed that she had the real answer to a long, happy marriage. The wife has to be a saint and have lots of patience.

Grumpiness

Part of being patient is to tolerate your spouse's grumpiness. Everyone is grumpy once in awhile.

Pat said, "Why are you so grumpy?"

"I'm not grumpy. You're the one who's grumpy," I replied.

"Boy, you really are grumpy, aren't you?" she said.

"No, you're really grumpy," I said.

"I guess we're both grumpy," she said. Matter settled.

A Bad Day

Not every day of marriage is filled with roses and champagne and good feelings. I recall when I had a bad day. I was grumpy, moody, and nasty to Pat all day. I realized that I was being a terrible grump, but there seemed to be nothing I could do about it. I snarled at the slightest provocation. Everything seemed to go wrong, and even if it didn't go wrong, I was convinced that it did.

The next day, I apologized to Pat. I said, "I'm sorry that I was so grumpy, nasty, and moody yesterday." Her response was, "I didn't notice any difference. That's the way you are most of the time."

The way to improve behavior is to think about what you are doing and saying, and convince yourself that you should be nice to others, no matter what.

Actually, I like to be grumpy. It attracts Pat's attention. Here's a poem that tells about another way to overcome grumpiness:

The Grump

I am a grump.
I'm nasty and mean,
I'm the grumpiest grump
That's ever been seen.

When someone says "yes"
I always say "no,"
I'm a negative grump
Wherever I go.

I complain about everything,
Nothing is right
I make people miserable,
That's my delight.

3. Glum grump drawing.

Someone suggested
That I try to smile,
I think I will try
But it may take awhile.

I'll stretch my lips
In an upward direction,
I'll practice a smile
'Til it reaches perfection.

4. Smiling grump drawing.

My face looks so strange,
My lips now are curled,
My teeth are exposed,
As I smile at the world.

Hey, I never knew
That a smile feels so good,
I'm losing my grumps,
They told me I would.

My whole life is changed now,
I've learned a new style,
I'm no longer a grump,
'Cause I know how to smile.

How true!

Conflicts

It's sometimes difficult to live with another person. Conflicts are certain to arise. Arguments are a normal part of every marriage. In the old days, married couples negotiated and resolved their conflicts. Nowadays, after a few arguments, couples may get divorced.

Every married couple has arguments in the car. We decided that arguments in the car don't count. Backseat driving is acceptable. In my case it's desirable since, whenever I turn the key to start the car, I turn off my mind. Pat refers to this condition as "mindless driving." I need continuous guidance while driving.

Whenever we go somewhere in the car, I'm usually behind the wheel, but Pat is next to me and is really driving the car. "Watch out!" "Why did you turn so sharply?" "Slow down." "Why did you make a left turn instead of a right turn?" "Watch out for those people crossing the street." "Don't hit that old lady." "Do you want to go through that truck in front of you?" "After all these years, don't you know how to drive a car?" "Why do you zoom up to the red light?" "Why don't you go a little faster, so that you can get a speeding ticket?"

We argue regularly in the car. Once I was driving and Pat became so angry that that she jumped out of the car . . . while it was still moving.

The secret for maintaining good relations is to forget adverse comments immediately after getting out of the car.

A Traffic Tale

One day, I received a frantic phone call from Pat. "I fell asleep and drove into a ditch," she said. My immediate response was, "Is the car okay?" It never occurred to me to ask if she was okay. I guess I thought she was okay, since she was talking to me on the phone and wasn't dead. Even I was surprised that the condition of the car was the first thing that came to my mind.

As pedestrians, whenever we cross the street illegally in heavy traffic, I always say to Pat, "Don't worry. They're not allowed to hit us."

Silent Arguments

The good news is that arguments change in their nature as a marriage goes on. After more than fifty-two years of marriage, we learned to have silent arguments. I know what upsets her, and she knows what upsets me. When conflicts arise, we have a few minutes of heavy silence and grim facial expressions. Then it's over, and feelings of love return, and we forget what we were angry about in the first place. We came to realize that it doesn't pay to yell and scream at each other. We know that we won't get divorced because of an argument, so why bother wasting all that energy? If nations would adopt the same philosophy and realize that years after a war, they would be good friends, why bother to have the war?

Household Chores

I do very few chores around the house. Whenever Pat asks me to do something, I tell her, "I have more important things to do." I also tell her, "I'm paid to think."

I am inept at mechanical things. I need an assistant for everything that I do. I once had to ask Pat to help me screw in a lightbulb in the kitchen. Because I think so much, I am mechanically incompetent. Pat is very good at fixing things and assembling complicated devices. I attribute her skills to her experience in reading directions for sewing, knitting, quilting, and computing, and to good common sense. I seem to be lacking in these areas.

Garbage

I became accustomed to doing two chores at home, taking out the garbage on Monday nights and making the bed.

Pat used effective psychology to convince me to take out the garbage. At first, Pat would give me a firm command,

"Marvin, take out the garbage." Then her approach changed. "Marvin, do you want to take out the garbage now, or do you want to take it out later?" That strategy worked, and I regularly take out the garbage. I even enjoy it, since I can then see what Pat is throwing out.

I am not good at garbage. I have difficulty sorting out trash from recyclables. I don't know whether or not a used pizza box or a particular piece of used aluminum foil should be recycled. Pat recycles everything. I just take out the garbage, no matter what.

Making the Bed

I make the bed each morning, but there seems to be no purpose in making the bed. This seems like a waste of time. Why bother to make the bed? Who will come to your house during the day and say, "I'd like to see your bed"? The next time you see the bed will be at night. Then you'll pull the covers down and get in. So why bother making it in the first place? But I compromise, and I make the bed.

Once when Pat got up in the middle of the night to go to the bathroom, I made the bed. My way of protesting.

She got even. One early morning, Pat took the sheets off the bed to wash them while I was still sleeping.

The Drip

One day Pat asked me to mow the lawn. Of course, I resisted. But when I noticed how shaggy the lawn appeared,

I decided to mow it. It was a hot, humid day and I sweated profusely. After completing this arduous task, I rushed up to the bathroom in our bedroom to take a shower. When I finished showering, I turned off the faucet but the water kept dripping. So I screamed for help from Pat. She turned the faucet knob until there were just a few drops coming from the faucet. I decided to make the knob even tighter, and I caused a steady stream of water that couldn't be stopped.

It was now nighttime, so we couldn't get the plumber. There was no shower shutoff valve in sight. The shutoff valve for the water to the entire house was in a precarious state. Many years ago, that faucet was leaking, and several plumbers unsuccessfully tried to repair it. Finally, an old, experienced plumber tied some string around the faucet and stopped the leak . . . for more than forty years. So I didn't want to touch that faucet, and we went to sleep with the sound of a waterfall in our bedroom. Neither of us got much sleep, in fear that we would be drowned. In the morning, Pat went down to the basement and found a separate shutoff valve for the shower. Saved again!

Cooking and Eating

Pat doesn't particularly like to cook, or even eat very much. I like to eat but not cook. My cooking skills include making hot dogs, baked potatoes, canned soup, cold cereal, and cheese grits. I got the cheese grits recipe from a friend in Georgia who claims that this recipe attracts beautiful women. Actually, that's true, since Pat likes my cheese grits.

Love and Marriage

We eat out in inexpensive restaurants and always ask for the senior discount. We had our fifty-first anniversary dinner in an inexpensive restaurant. The restaurant owner was so pleased that he came over to congratulate us, and he thanked us for celebrating our anniversary at his restaurant. I hate to spend money on fancy restaurants. Usually, fancy restaurants serve small amounts of elegant food on large plates. The salad often has a variety of leaves that, as a biologist, I can't identify. I like restaurants that overfill plates with two meals worth of real food. Some restaurants we patronize are so inexpensive that they practically pay us to eat there.

We also use discount coupons whenever we can. One of my hobbies is to cut coupons out of the Sunday newspaper. "Buy one, get one free" is my favorite discount coupon. I'll go out of my way to use these coupons, even if I don't like the food item that's advertised. Oftentimes, I'll "buy one," and Pat will buy something else that she really likes, but that isn't eligible for the discount. It's also very disappointing when, at the last minute, I read the nearly invisible expiration date on the coupon and discover that the coupon has expired. Be sure you check the expiration dates on your coupons before you offer to take your spouse out to an expensive dinner.

Paper Napkins

Whenever we ate in an inexpensive restaurant that had paper napkins, I would ask the waiter. "May we have some more napkins? She's a sloppy eater." The waiter's usual reaction was, "I think I know who the sloppy eater is." In response to my rude remark, one waitress gave Pat several napkins and said, "I gave her the extra napkins so that she can clean you up after you eat." In another instance, the waitress didn't say anything. She simply gave Pat one extra napkin, and gave me two. Lately, whenever I ask for an extra napkin, I say, "I'm a sloppy eater." This tactic avoids a silent argument.

Pat says that she cooked for many years, and now she wants to rest for many years. When we do eat at home, Pat often serves some sort of mixture of rice, chicken, and vegetables. Sometimes I can't recognize the ingredients. It seems that we are always eating leftovers, but I never see the original food. This comment leads to the threat, "You can do the cooking from now on." I have learned to resist making that comment, and have avoided cooking meals.

Marvelous Meals

Our daughter studied dietetics, and she told us how to make foods tasty and appealing. A primary factor is color. Oranges, greens, reds, yellows, and browns make the meal more attractive and palatable. One night, Pat was busy making a chicken and potato dish. She called out, "Marvin, it's time for dinner." I sat down at the table and Pat put my meal in front of me. It was a plain, bland chicken breast and a wrinkled, overcooked baked potato. The food looked colorless and unappealing. Pat sensed my displeasure and announced, "I wasn't thinking much about dinner for us tonight." I agreed with her remark, but said nothing for fear that I might end up doing the cooking from then on.

When we eat at home, we have a magic dishwasher. I put my dirty dishes in the sink and, the next day, they magically appear, clean and sparkling, in the dish cabinet. There must be some goblin that takes care of the dishes. As long as this keeps happening, I won't ask any questions.

Occasionally, we invite guests to our home for dinner. After dinner, a guest will always ask, "Can I help with the dishes?" I reply, "No. That's okay. Pat will take care of it." A silent argument follows.

We rarely have dessert, but Pat is a cookie monster. She devours any cookie that comes into view. I sometimes think that she prefers cookies to me. Her obsession with cookies inspired me to write this poem:

The Cookie Man

I am the cookie man,
I eat as many as I can,
There never is an end,
Every cookie is my friend.

Chocolate and vanilla too,
It doesn't matter which I chew,
When they see me they run away,
'Cause I will eat them if they stay.

Rebellion

At first, I accepted all criticisms and suggestions passively. Then I started fighting back with snippy remarks. For example, "Marvin, why did you make that left turn?" My response: "I made the left turn so that I could go around the block once before making a right turn." Or, "Marvin, you almost hit that lady." My response: "I saw her. I know that I'm not allowed to hit anyone with the car. She was crossing quickly enough for me to miss her." Or, "Marvin, you left your jacket on the chair." My response: "I left it there deliberately to test the honesty of people in the restaurant." This approach did not work too well, so I went back to shutting my mouth: a wise decision that has contributed to a long, happy marriage.

Giving and Saving

Pat is a "giver" and I am a "saver." Pat throws out almost anything that might be perceived as "cluttering the house," while I cling to the minutes of a meeting that I attended in 1970, just in case I need that information sometime.

I save many shoes, pants, and shirts that no longer fit me. I save them in case I lose weight someday and can fit into them once again. One day, I discovered that Pat gave away some of my clothes without conferring with me . . . and I'm not even dead yet.

My office is a great example of "saving." Piles of papers and books, photos of Pat and family, and miscellaneous

5. Marvin in his highly organized office. Photo by Steve Sartori.

memorabilia surround me. I occasionally have avalanches, when papers and books tumble from the table into a garbage bin on the floor; I retrieve these valuable items but am often tempted to leave them there. I wonder about earthquakes in Syracuse.

Generosity

Pat is a very generous, caring woman. She donates money to many worthy causes.

I once received a leather portfolio in the mail from a radio station where I had been interviewed. "How nice," I thought, "they liked my interview so much that they gave

21

me a gift." That wasn't why they sent me the gift. Pat had donated $500 to the radio station—and we couldn't even get the station on the air.

We were in New York City and went to the Joyce dance theater. I opened the program book, and our generous donation to the theater was acknowledged. I said to Pat, "But we only go to this theater once a year. Why are we donating money?" She replied, "We have to support the arts." I thought to myself, "We don't have to support the arts all over the world." But I said nothing aloud.

Before she retired, Pat was an administrator in the Writing Program at Syracuse University. One winter day, a student entered her office wearing a thin jacket. Pat reminded her that this was Syracuse and it was cold outside. Pat asked, "Why don't you put on your winter coat?" The young lady explained that she was a poor orphan from California, and that she could not afford to buy a coat. Pat promptly bought her one and helped her get a part-time job on campus. I didn't tell that story to my students for fear that they would be coming to my office during the winter, wearing thin jackets, and lamenting that they couldn't afford to buy a winter coat.

Another time, Pat handed me a large, plastic bag full of "stuff," and asked me to deliver the bag to the Rescue Mission. While driving there, I began to wonder, "What's in this bag?" I opened the bag and found it full of perfectly usable towels. I took them back and gave them to my son for mopping up his children's regurgitations.

Now whenever Pat gives me something to donate, I put it in the trunk of my car. She thinks that she has made a charitable donation, but I know that I have saved some valuable possessions. So both of us are winners.

Another time, Pat donated some of my favorite children's books to a local school without asking my permission. I was silently angry. I told her that she could give away all my possessions after I die but not now. The next day, we were scheduled to go on a four-day trip to visit high schools. I apologized to Pat. "I'm sorry," I said, "I don't want to sit in the car with you for four days and not talk."

She replied, "Why not? That would be good."

I sometimes think about having a garage sale some day, but not until I am convinced that I really don't need the items. That day may never come.

My Shoes

One day, we had a discussion about my shoes in the closets. Pat claimed that I had many pairs of shoes that I haven't worn for twenty years and am not likely to ever wear again. Of course, I wanted to save the shoes, just in case I needed them someday. After an intensive "discussion," Pat went upstairs to the bedroom. When I went up there, I found the bed covered with all my shoes from the closets. "Try these all on," she said. I did, and I defended the need for each pair of shoes. Finally, I agreed to give up three pairs of old shoes that had worn soles and heels and were 1950s styles. I also discovered a pair of new, unworn shoes. I had bought the same pair of shoes twice. Shoe store owners love to have me visit their shop. A reasonable guideline would be, "If you haven't used something in more than twenty years, get rid of it. You really don't need it."

My Missing Things

I am constantly missing things. "Pat, I can't find my bathing suit. Someone must have borrowed it." Or "I can't find my red sweater. Did you give it away?" or "Pat, there's no ketchup." "Where are the books that I left on the kitchen table? I was going to work there." "My keys are missing. Someone must have stolen them." It is truly amazing that Pat can find most things that I am missing. She is a miracle worker.

The Valentine's Day Card

In my lifetime, I have always tried to practice parsimony. I am the product of a very poor childhood, and I have difficulty being too generous. As an example, on Valentine's Day, I used to browse through Valentine's Day cards in the store. When I saw one that I liked, I said to Pat, "If I was going to buy you a card, this is the one I'd choose."

Then I adopted a new practice. I bought a large Valentine's Day card with a picture of a bear inside. The outside of the card says, "How much do I love you?" When the card is opened, the bear's arms stretch out and the caption says, "This much."

After Valentine's Day, I put the card in the closet, and I give her the same card the next year. She always forgets the card that I gave her last year, so this practice works well and saves a lot of card money. What's the point of buying cards in the first place for any occasion? We read the card, and then throw it away.

The Pre-Memorial Fund

Pat's ultimate generosity came when Syracuse University was building a new biology building. Pat wanted to have my name put on a room in the new building. She donated a large sum of money to initiate the "Marvin Druger Recognition Fund." Since I have taught more than 40,000 students in my career, Pat felt that many former students would contribute to the fund.

Actually, I had jokingly suggested to a development officer that they initiate a "Marvin Druger Pre-Memorial Fund." I told him that I had been at Syracuse University for forty-five years and, when I died, the university would probably establish a fund in my memory. I said, "I want to have the fund while I'm alive, so that I can find out who gives and how much."

While I was telling the development officer this, he had a slight smile on his face. I stopped my dialogue abruptly and said, "I know what you're thinking. I'm worth more dead than alive." He broke into a hearty laugh. That's exactly what he was thinking.

Pat actually did establish the fund. What was named after me would depend on how much money was raised. I told everyone that they might raise so little money that I'd have the urinal in the men's room named after me. I told this to one lady, and she replied, "It's better to have your name on a urinal when you are alive than on a water fountain when you are dead." A wise thought. Actually, enough money was raised to have two plaques on the outside of one of the biology teaching laboratories in the new life sciences building that identifies the "Marvin Druger Introductory Biology Laboratory."

Besides giving to all sorts of charitable causes, Pat established savings funds for college expenses of our grandchildren. She even gave a large sum of money to our grown children. One contribution was to pay off school loans of my son who is an ophthalmologist. Another contribution was to help finance a major household renovation for my other son and his wife. Once they received that money, they increased the extent of the renovation and it cost them more than it would have without our contribution. Pat also bought an expensive, automatic fireplace for our daughter. Pat explained that she wants to see our children enjoy our money now, rather than inherit it. I actually have a lot of enjoyment from Pat's generosity. Donate your money to your children before you die, so that you can enjoy watching them spend it. This is an

interesting approach that you may want to consider.

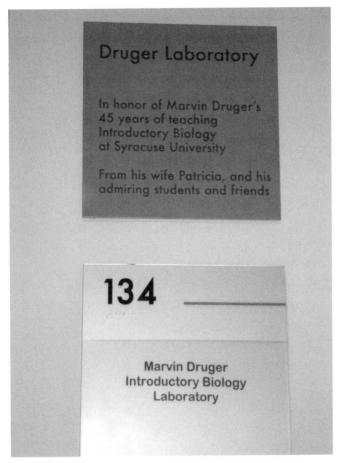

6. The Marvin Druger Introductory Biology Laboratory plaques.

Because of our many donations, our names are engraved on a campus bench, a campus tree, a brick in the Orange Grove patio, two chairs in the Setnor Auditorium in the School of Music, an elevator in the Erie

Canal Museum, and two chairs in the Merry-Go-Round Theater in Auburn, New York. I made sure that her chair was on the left and mine was on the right, since that's the way we sleep in our bed at home. Pat also donated money to renovate a conference room in Jowonio School, an inclusive preschool in Syracuse. A large sign over the entrance to the room reads: "Druger Family Community Room." When requests for donations arrive in the mail, I am tempted to tear them up before Pat sees them . . . but . . . for some reason, I don't.

The good news is that my name appears on all of Pat's donations. Whenever I question a particular donation, Pat says, "I'm making you a generous man." That's true.

Whenever I raise the possibility of leaving some money for us, Pat asks, "What do you need that you don't have?" A good question that I find difficult to answer.

I'm reluctant to confess that it feels good to donate to worthy causes. It's gratifying to know that you are helping other human beings in some way.

Pat's Creations

Pat lives a life of thoughtfulness, caring, and giving. She does tax returns for AARP, she is a volunteer docent at the Erie Canal Museum in Syracuse, she is on the board of Friends of Jowonio School, she donates money to many worthy causes, she volunteers to help others whenever help is needed.

7. Marvin outside the door of the Druger Family Community Room at Jowonio preschool in Syracuse.

Pat is a talented seamstress. She sews many wonderful items—and gives them away. One day, I had a great idea. Why not start a business and sell these items? Pat strongly objected to this suggestion. I told her that she would not have to sit at the sewing machine and make these items. We would do it the American way. We would outsource the jobs to workers in other countries who would make the items for very low wages. Finally, to encourage her to start a business, I purchased 500 business cards for her that advertised "Pat's Creations." She was not happy with this gift, especially since the sewing machine emblem on the card was backwards. That didn't help my cause. She still gives her beautiful creations away for free. I was at a charity auction where many items were displayed. All the items I looked at and wanted to bid on were made and donated by Pat.

The Perfect Marriage

When I was president of the National Science Teachers Association, I traveled extensively. I was away so often that, when I was home, Pat felt like I was an intruder. She was beginning to doubt my existence. Pat actually enjoyed my absence. "It's the perfect marriage," she said. "I never slept better. I miss you when you're away, but I can't wait until you leave." I'm sure that many of you have similar feelings after a prolonged visit by distant family members.

Animal Lovers

Pat and I have mixed feelings about having cats or dogs as pets. They have to be pampered, they poop and pee, they don't grow up and become independent like children, they have to be cared for when you leave town, they bark, they shed hair, they require costly medical care, and they are under your feet no matter where you walk in the house. On the other hand, dogs give anyone unlimited love and affection. There is something warm and passionate about having a dog shlurp your face with its tongue.

The cocker spaniel that my family owned when I was a child came with a pedigree. Lady Resurgum Ballad was the mother and Shooting-Box-This-Away was the father. I discovered that when you buy a dog, you get a pedigree of the dog's ancestry. When you get married, you don't get anything.

As an adult, my main reason for not owning a dog is that they usually die within your lifetime. I couldn't bear the death of my favorite pet, so Pat bought me a wooden Dalmatian, named Spot. We also own a stuffed monkey, named Bobo.

My favorite pet is a Saguaro cactus that I planted from seed more than fifteen years ago. It requires virtually no care except a dash of water now and then. It doesn't bark and it doesn't pee or poop. I don't worry about it when we go on a trip. In about seventy-five years, it will grow its first

8. Pat and Marvin's pets: Saguaro, Bobo (*left*), and Spot.

arm. It lives about 150 years, so it will be mourning over me. What pet could be more appealing?

Her Favorite Animal

We were visiting an elementary school in Costa Rica. The children were delightful, and we had a stimulating conversation about animals with them. One child asked my wife, "What's your favorite animal?" My wife thought for a second and replied, "My husband." It's so nice to be loved.

Slips of the Tongue

Very often, words come out of our mouths without being processed by our brains. I am famous for such "Marvin-isms." It's sometimes difficult for me to talk and think at the same time. The problem is that, once the words leave your mouth, you can't get them back again. It's important to think before you speak.

Many people think that I resemble Hugh Hefner of *Playboy* magazine fame. I was once sitting at an airport with Pat when a lady came over to me and said, "Pardon me. But are you Hugh Hefner?" Without thinking, I said, "If I was Hugh Hefner, would I be sitting next to this old, gray-haired lady?" This was an immediate cause of a silent argument that lasted until the evening.

I told that story to a student and she said, "You should have said 'great-haired woman.'" Good idea . . . for next time.

A student invited Pat and me to dinner at her apartment with her mother and her sister. Her mother worked at a beauty salon and she gave Pat a bottle of very expensive exfoliant cream from Barcelona, Spain. Pat tried it the next day. I looked at her and exclaimed, "Wow! That stuff really made your face look much better." From the mouth of babes . . .

I boasted to a friend, "We've been married fifty-three years!" Pat corrected me. "No, it's fifty-two years." My quick reply: "Well, it seems like fifty-three."

9. Pat's naturally "great" hair. Photo by Steve Sartori.

Someone said to me, "Your wife is old, but she's pretty." I responded, "Yes. She's pretty old."

On the other hand, without thinking, we sometimes say words that have positive effects. Pat was telling me what her divorced friends said about their ex-husbands: "My husband spoke in paragraphs." "My husband walked like a duck."

Without thinking, the words that came out of my mouth were, "There's nothing I don't like about you." I couldn't have done better if I had used my brain to think of those words. That was a winner.

Pat and I were discussing an important decision that had to be made. I said, "We have to think about this decision." She remarked, "Yes, but thinking is not one of your strong points." She made the decision, and it was the correct one.

One day, Pat was locking the door as she was leaving the house. I backed the car out of the garage and stopped just outside the door near a bunch of rocks. The car was too far back, and Pat couldn't easily get in. She yelled, "Why don't you use your head?"

I replied, "For what?"

"How about for thinking," she exclaimed. Another example of thinking not being one of my strong points.

More Mouth Leaks

Pat and I were having dinner in a restaurant with a friend and her new boyfriend. Our conversation turned to the Syracuse University basketball team. "Most of the players I've had in my class are really bright," I said, "But JJ was not the least bit interested in using any brainpower for academics."

The boyfriend looked surprised. "JJ is my brother."

I felt like crawling under the table. This incident taught me to speak no evil of anyone to anyone, especially if you don't know the anyone well.

Another mouth leak occurred when Pat and I were driving into a state park and I noticed a sign that said that the admission price was $7, but seniors were admitted free. My daughter was driving a van with kids behind my car. I asked Pat to get out of the car and drive my daughter's car, so that they wouldn't have to pay the entrance fee. Pat refused, but I finally forced her out of the car, and she got behind the wheel of my daughter's van. When I reached the entrance gate, it was obvious to the ticket agent that I was a senior. I wanted to explain Pat's situation in the van behind me. I said, "The lady that's driving the van behind me doesn't have her driver's license with her, but she looks much older than she is." I meant to say, "She's much older than she looks." Pat found out about this remark, and I paid a much higher price that evening than I would have if I simply paid the park entrance fee.

Liberation

Married couples generally share things. I have difficulty sharing anything with anyone. This may be a throwback to my poor childhood. Pat wants me to share in household chores. I'm resistant. "Pat, there's no ketchup on the table," I said. She replied, "So go get the ketchup." Even though she sat closer to the refrigerator, she refused to get the ketchup for me.

When Pat retired from her administrative position at Syracuse University, I hired her to be my part-time secretary. She was sitting in my outer office and I said, "Pat, can you please make two copies of this article for me?"

She replied, "I'm busy. Do it yourself."

The next day I asked her to do something for me in the afternoon. I found some time in the morning, so I did the task. She sat me down and scolded, "If you ask me to do something and I say that I will do it, then *you* don't do it."

I decided that this was not my idea of a secretary. Since then, I have a poster-sized photo of her hanging on a wall in my office, and she works for me at home.

The "Clean-Its"

Periodically, Pat gets the "clean-its." All closets and cabinets have to be cleaned out. Anything that isn't used daily becomes a victim of the "clean-its." When in doubt, throw it out. What is not discarded gets neatly put away somewhere. It's comforting to know that, even if I can't find my razor, it's stored neatly somewhere. The somewhere is soon forgotten. There's always too much junk lying around. There's never seems to be enough room in the house. "Room for what?" I wonder.

One day, Pat cleared books from a large bookcase. "Why are you doing that?" I asked.

"We need room for books," she replied. That's what we had on the shelves in the first place. I couldn't figure that one out.

Dryer Episodes

Pat asked me to put the basket of clothing into the dryer in the basement. The next morning, Pat noticed that the clothes were still wet. "What happened?" she asked, "Why didn't the clothes dry?" I had no clue. Maybe it was because she never told me to switch on the dryer?

When Pat was immobilized in bed because of a back infection, I was obliged to do all the household chores. I knew so little about the house that I had to ask Pat where the gas meter was. One of my chores was doing the laundry. I put the laundered clothes into the dryer (this time I turned it on) and the clothes did not get dry. I yelled to Pat that I was going to buy a new dryer. "What do I do with the old one?" I asked at the store.

"For $10 we'll take it away. For nothing, we'll put it on the street for the sanitation workers to take it away."

Naturally, I wanted to save $10, so I had them install the new dryer and put the old one on the curb. While I was in the basement the next morning, Pat yelled down to me, "Where are my velour pants?"

It turned out that they were in the discarded dryer, along with an assortment of our best-liked clothing. I ran outside, but the dryer was gone. I called the sanitation department, and they sent a jeep out on the dump but couldn't find the dryer. Some scavenger must have driven by, spotted a dryer, and took it—filled with our favorite clothing.

The next day, I discovered that lint had clogged the vent from the dryer. Nobody ever said that I had to clean out the lint. The old dryer was perfectly good.

Sewing

Pat always had great talent for sewing, quilting, and crafts. One day, she decided to create a necktie for me. She bought material and spent some time sewing the tie together. I didn't like the tie, and I told her so. She became angry and took her scissors and cut the tie in half—while it was on my neck. I wondered what she was really aiming for.

Another day, I noticed a small hole in the front of my sweater. I was going to ask Pat to sew it, but I decided that I could handle the problem myself. I got out a sewing kit, threaded the needle, and sewed the hole in the sweater while wearing it. I soon discovered that I had sewn the sweater to my tie.

A Cure for an Injured Shoulder

Pat injured her shoulder while lifting weights. I was concerned. "I wish I could help you," I said.

She responded, "Stop talking so much. That would help."

The Boating Safety Exam

Pat and I took a boating safety course together. The instructor was terrible. Once, while lecturing, he suddenly announced, "I have a cramp in my leg." He sat down, and the entire class stood up and left the room.

We had to take a final exam on boating safety. I studied intensively. Pat never opened the book. We had dinner before the exam, and I told her what I thought might be on the test. I was very apprehensive about it. I was afraid that she would pass and I would fail. My stomach dropped and I started to sweat when Pat was the first one in the class to hand in her completed exam. My worst fears were realized. But luck was with me. I got three wrong, and Pat got five wrong. Ha, ha!

The Bench, the Tree, the Chairs, and the Brick

One day, when I was walking on the Syracuse University campus, I met the new chancellor. We chatted, and he commented, "Nice campus we have here."

I replied, "Yes, but there's no place to sit down. There are no benches."

He said, "That's a good idea. We'll put it in the plan."

A few months later, the school newspaper announced that benches were going to be placed on the campus. I immediately wrote a letter to the chancellor and stated, "I've been here for a long time. When I die, people will probably contribute money to have a bench named in my honor. I'd like to have the bench while I'm alive, so that if someone I don't like is sitting on my bench, I can say, 'Get the hell off my bench.'"

Apparently, my letter was well received, and we were allowed to make a donation to get our names on a bench. I spent many hours that winter standing in various spots on campus to decide the best site for the "Druger bench." I finally picked a spot outside the building where I gave my biology lectures. We had a "bench-warming" ceremony with punch and cookies for everyone in attendance. The chancellor cut a red ribbon, and the bench had a small plaque that said, "Donated by Patricia and Marvin Druger. For our friends at Syracuse University."

The next day, I went to see our bench, and it was gone. Someone had thrown it against the wall of the building and cracked it. A replacement bench was obtained, and now all the benches on campus are bolted to the ground.

At graduation time, two old ladies were sitting on the bench. I approached them and proudly announced, "That's my bench." The response was, "Oh, do we have to get off?"

While sitting on the bench one day, I thought how nice it would be to have a "Druger tree" to shade people who sit on the bench. I asked the university administrator in charge of these matters if we could make a donation to have a tree. He responded, "If I knew you could afford a tree, I would have charged you more for the bench."

This administrator resigned and was replaced by a botanist from Cornell University. I became friendly with him, and he allowed us to make a donation to plant a tree. The stick-like tree was planted across the path from the bench. The plaque under the tree read, "Donated by Patricia and Marvin Druger. To shade our friends who sit on the bench."

It soon became obvious that the sun went the wrong way and the tree would not shade the bench. So we changed the plaque to read, "Donated by Patricia and Marvin Druger. In celebration of our many years at Syracuse."

10. Pat and Marvin planting their sticklike tree opposite the Druger bench. Photo by Steve Sartori.

11. Pat, the tree, and Marvin. Photo by Steve Sartori.

12. The Druger Bench and Tree on the Syracuse University main campus in 2009.

The Brick

On the occasion of our forty-sixth wedding anniversary, I was hard-pressed to think of an anniversary gift for Pat. After many birthdays and anniversaries, it becomes difficult to think of a gift that hasn't already been given. This was not a problem for Pat. She always gave me a sweater for my birthday. One year, I awoke early on my birthday and wondered what Pat had gotten for me. "I'll bet it's another sweater," I thought. I was wrong. Pat gave me two sweaters for that birthday. Having a lot of sweaters is very important in the winter, even though I wear the same one almost all the time.

I had a brainstorm about what to get Pat for our forty-sixth wedding anniversary. Syracuse University was establishing the "Orange Grove" on the main campus. A donation would buy an engraved brick. So I made a donation from my personal funds and bought Pat a brick that was supposed to say, "Patricia and Marvin Druger. In celebration of 46 years of love and marriage." I wanted to tell Pat about the brick on the day of our anniversary, but we were having a silent argument that day. When I told her about the brick the next day, she said, "That's nice. But if you said forty-six years on the engraving, you'll have to buy me a new brick each year." I quickly had the engraving changed to "Patricia and Marvin Druger. In celebration of many years of love and marriage."

My goal in retirement is to follow Pat around all day. She does wonderful things for people, and maybe some of

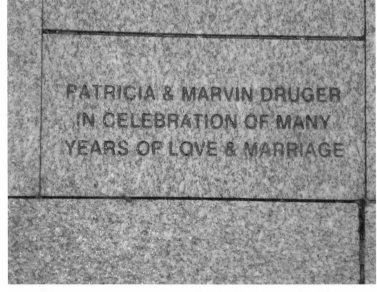

13. The forty-sixth anniversary engraved brick in the Orange Grove on the Syracuse University main campus.

her "giving" approach to life will rub off on me. I told this goal to Pat and, for some reason, she didn't think this plan would work well.

The Dance Contest

We attended the wedding of one of my graduate students. The master of ceremonies organized an interesting dance contest. He had everyone on the dance floor to start. Then couples would sit down, according to how long they had been married. "Couples married less than ten years, please

46

sit down. Couples married less than twenty years, please sit down," and so forth. The goal was to have the couple married the longest still dancing at the end. When the game reached couples married more than forty-five years, I thought our fate was sealed. The other three couples looked much older than us. Surely, they had been married much longer. In the end, we won. The older couples had been married more than once, and we were the only surviving couple that had been married to each other for more than forty-five years. We proudly continued dancing alone on the dance floor.

14. Marvin whispering sweet nothings in Pat's ear as they dance to victory in the marriage longevity dance contest at a friend's wedding. Photo by Douglas Lloyd, www.douglaslloyd.com.

Our Combined 125th Birthday Party

Pat and I decided to celebrate our combined 125 years of living by hosting a birthday party at a local banquet hall. Everyone was trying to figure out each of our ages. My usual comment was, "Doesn't she look great for eighty-five?" We invited everyone we could think of. Pat and I disagreed about bringing birthday presents. She didn't want any. I settled the matter by writing a poem on the invitation:

> Birthdays are great,
> Parties are fun,
> Pat says, "No presents,"
> But Marvin wants one.

15. A large, decorated cake made for Pat and Marvin's combined 125th birthday party at Drumlins Country Club in Syracuse.

So, if you bring a gift,
Don't spend much money,
Get something that's cheap and funny.

We received many inexpensive, creative presents and the affair was a great success. I stood on a chair for about an hour and told jokes. We hope that we can have our combined 200th birthday party in the future. The combined birthday party saves time and money, as compared to individual birthday parties. Try it and see.

Our Fiftieth Anniversary

We were thrilled to receive two toilets for our lake house as a fiftieth anniversary gift from our children. I think fondly of our children every time I go to the bathroom at the lake house.

It was especially difficult to think of a fiftieth anniversary gift for Pat. First of all, she has everything she needs. Second, fiftieth is the "golden" anniversary, and, considering the high price of gold, a fortune might be spent on a gift. So I wrote her a poem and mounted it in a gold-colored frame from the Dollar Store. This saved a lot of money.

To My Wife Pat

We've been married fifty years
And I am pleased to say
That the love that we have shared
Grows stronger every day.

We've shared so many things,
And we've had so much fun,
Our special traits are different,
But in spirit we are one.

Love and friendship last forever,
They never fade away,
We walk and talk together
And we laugh at life each day.

Fifty years have passed,
They went by very fast,
But our love stays young,
And forever it will last.

Happy Fiftieth Anniversary!

I read this poem to many people. They usually asked, "Did she cry?" Actually, she didn't cry. She said, "What are you trying to do, show off?" She knew that I would be trying to impress people with what a nice husband I was. After so many years of years of marriage, she knows me well.

Our Fifty-second Anniversary

After my success in saving money on a gift for our fiftieth anniversary, I decided to do the same for our fifty-second anniversary, and I wrote another poem to Pat:

To Pat on Our 52nd Anniversary

52 is special,
It's one more than 51,
It's one less than 53,
And it's the only one.

We'll celebrate 52,
'Cause that's how many years
That we have been together,
And shared each other's cares.

Living life together,
Laughing every day,
Making precious memories
That time can't take away.

Your ways of life are wonderful,
Your beauty makes you glow,
With your happy, caring manner,
You're the very best I know.

So, happy anniversary,
It's number 52,
I've been very lucky
To have shared my life with you

Pat's immediate response to this poem was, "I know!"

2 The Younger Days

Memories of our younger days fade and become jumbled as we grow older. Why we remember certain experiences and not others is a mystery, but here are some that I recall vividly.

Home Life

My father was a hard-working truck driver who only completed sixth grade, and my mother was a housewife with little formal education. My father drank beer, smoked cigars, and was a member of the Teamsters' Union. When he went to the polls to vote, someone stood outside the polling area and told him who to vote for—or else. He injured his back and had to depend upon the union to get food. I remember riding on the subway with him carrying a bag of food given to him by the union. I asked him what it was all about, and he looked ashamed and said nothing.

We lived on Forty-fourth Street in Brooklyn. Our window looked out on the elevated subway line, and the noise of trains was a regular feature of my childhood. My mother, father, older sister, and two younger brothers were crowded into a small apartment. Cockroaches and mice also lived with us. We were very poor, but, somehow, there was always food in the refrigerator.

My older sister had many girlfriends, and I tended to follow them around. I learned how to get along with girls from them. My youngest brother earned a Ph.D. in physics at the University of Rochester, and my other brother earned a master's degree at City College. I earned a bachelor's degree from Brooklyn College and master's and Ph.D. degrees from Columbia University. We went our separate ways. My sister never had the opportunity to attend college.

The Wildcats

My best friends were BZ and Junior. They lived nearby, and we formed a gang of about ten neighborhood boys called the Wildcats. We somehow managed to get enough money to buy purple jackets and we even rented a basement clubroom. The Wildcats were the pride of Abe's billiard parlor, and he had our group photo hanging on the wall. The poolroom was full of real gangsters, with guns and knives. But our gang was a good gang. We didn't drink, smoke, or care about girls. We played punchball, basketball, and stickball, and we tried to preserve our bodies for athletics. We did well in school and earned good grades.

16. Some of the Wildcat gang members as adults making their way in life. *Front row, left to right:* Marvin Druger, Ronald Kronheim, Gerson Sparer; *back row, left to right:* Irwin Davidson, Carl Helman, Martin Schubert, George Carson.

My parents liked me to get good grades, but there was no intellectual climate in our home. In those days, after high school, you went to *work* to support the family. Because my older sister went to work when she graduated high school, I didn't *have* to go to work. I asked my friends BZ and Junior what they were going to do when they graduated high school. "We're going to college" was the reply. "It's free."

"If it's free, then I'll go too." I was valedictorian of my high school graduating class, so I easily qualified for college entrance and I attended Brooklyn College. I earned a B in the first semester of the introductory biology course, and an A in the second semester. The faculty member sent me a note at the end of the second semester congratulating me on my excellent work. I was encouraged to take more biology courses, majored in biology, minored in science education, and graduated magna cum laude.

I was on the New Utrecht High School basketball team and then on the freshman basketball team at Brooklyn College. We played Erasmus High School the year they won the national championship. In the days when players did not dunk the ball, Erasmus players dunked the ball, time and time again. We lost 93-2. Near the end of the game, the coach finally put me in the game. I was free under the basket, frantically waving to our point guard, Art, to throw me the ball. He didn't.

The coach called a time-out. "Art," he said, "you saw Druger free under the basket. Why didn't you throw him the ball?"

Art replied, "He wouldn't have made the shot anyhow."

I was on the freshman basketball team at Brooklyn College. I learned that being on a college sports team was very time consuming. We practiced from 5 to 8 P.M. every night, and even when I found some time to do homework, I was too tired to put in my maximum effort. I realized that I would never make the NBA, and I quit the team after one year. My grades improved. Since then, I've had great empathy for college athletes. It's difficult to be on a sports team and take the same courses nonathletes take and achieve at a high level.

Teaching at Columbia University

I was a graduate student in zoology at Columbia University, and I was told that I would be teaching the evening course in zoology to adult students who were coming back to school to enter medical school or some new profession. I looked for the professor who was in charge of the day course. I entered a lab and saw a short, energetic scientist in a lab coat. He spotted me and said, "So, you're Druger. Here's the book." Fortunately, I had previous teaching experience at Brooklyn College and as a student teacher, but I never forgot this abrupt introduction to teaching at Columbia.

I had two assistants who were senior Ph.D. students, Sasha and Shelley. They constantly tried to rattle me. I once told the class that *Cerebratulus* (a worm) was the first organism to have a true anus. This characterized an efficient, one-way digestive tract. Shelly interrupted my talk, "Did *Cerebratulus really* have an anus?" This harassment was a regular feature of my classes, but it was all in fun.

Cheating

And then there was the cheating incident. Giles was teaching an undergraduate zoology course and he prided himself on preventing cheating in his course. One evening,

I helped him proctor the exam. A student asked, "Can I go to the bathroom?" I asked Giles, who was dressed in a dark suit and a vest with a watch chain with a Phi Beta Kappa key dangling from his vest pocket. He thought a minute, and then climbed on top of one of the lab tables and announced, "Any of you men have to go to the john? Follow me!" And he marched them to the men's room.

Weeks later, the student who asked to leave the room told me in confidence that he had cheated. I said, "That's impossible. Nobody ever cheats in Giles' class." It turns out that when the student went to the bathroom, he picked up a paper with some answers that a previous student had pasted under the toilet seat in a stall. I was amazed, and I realized that if a student wants to cheat, there are ingenious ways it can be done and it's very difficult to control.

An attempt to cheat occurred while I was an undergraduate during a history exam in a large room, with proctors parading up and down the aisles. A fellow Wildcat gang member was sitting next to me. Suddenly, he stood up, covered his mouth and nose with a handkerchief and whispered, "What's the relation between church and state?" I looked up at him and laughed. Not only was he trying to cheat, but he was asking me an essay question. No way.

Part-Time Jobs

As a high school and college student, I had many part-time jobs. I hammered out numerals for golf bags from   57 scraps of leather, and I remember the grim expression of the old, full-time worker who was afraid I would replace him. I painted ceilings at a local A&P store, I sprinkled walnuts on fruitcakes at a bakery, I was a Western Union messenger, I was a salesman at a local clothing store, I was an usher at the Roxy Theater in New York City, and I was a camp counselor in the summers.

I somehow became the riflery instructor at the summer camp. Kids were lined up to shoot at paper targets. "Ready . . . aim . . . fire when ready" was my command. The kids shot in unison. "Okay, get your targets," I yelled. The kids all ran to get their targets. Bang! Another shot rang out as the kids were running to get their targets. One shooter hadn't yet gotten off his shot. Nobody was hurt, but I learned a lesson.

Another time, I arrived at the firing range to see the kids shooting at a porcupine in a tree. Fortunately, they missed the porcupine . . . and each other.

Leo was head counselor and an ex-Marine. He told me to stand a foot away from the target and tell him how he was doing. Bullets whizzed by my face and hit the target. Then we traded places, and fortunately my bullets whizzed by his face.

I was also designated as the overnight hike counselor. Several nights a week, I took kids into the hills to camp out for the night. Now you can understand my dislike for camping trips.

On one occasion, my family rode the rapids on the Green River out west. We camped out at night. I made sure that my family surrounded me in their sleeping bags so that wild animals would not attack me. I also sprayed the area around my sleeping bag with bug spray so that the insects would not get me. Pat pointed out, "Insects can fly and get you also." I never thought of that. Another lesson learned.

An old man and his two sons owned the clothing store that I worked in. One of the sons brought women to the store at night for romantic interludes. The other son objected and threatened to tell his brother's wife about what was going on. The reply from the promiscuous brother was, "Do you want to ruin a perfectly happy marriage?"

After graduating from Brooklyn College, I taught quantitative analysis for a year at Brooklyn Technical High School. I never had taken the course, and I learned the subject with the students. All the students in the school were boys, and they were bright students. It was a very successful experience, and I learned that I could learn new things if I really wanted to learn.

I also was a substitute teacher at a vocational high school. These were tough kids who were not intellectually oriented. I taught them the basics of sex to try to keep their interest. They seemed to know more about the subject than I did.

I was told that the most important thing to do was to carefully record attendance. If there was a robbery in the neighborhood, the attendance book could be used as a legal alibi for a student. Not much real teaching seemed to occur in the school. I saw one teacher throwing student papers into a wastebasket without even reading them.

One day, I noticed a boy sleeping with his head on the desk in the back of the classroom. I walked up to him and said, "What's the matter? Are you tired?"

He didn't move a muscle. His friend in the seat next to him said in a threatening voice, "Leave him alone; he's tired." I left him alone and walked away.

The manager of the Roxy Theater liked my voice, so he assigned me to the grand lobby of the theater. He told me to send people up to the balcony. "For the best remaining seats, use the stairway to the left," I repeated loudly. For variety, I would say, "Use the stairway to the left for the best remaining seats."

After an hour, the manager came to me enraged. "Druger, what the hell are you doing? The movie ended a half-hour ago. Everyone is in the balcony and there's nobody in the orchestra." He never told me to stop. Oh, well.

I used a yellow rope to block off one aisle in the theater. The comedian Morey Amsterdam came up to me and said, "What's the matter? Does that aisle have some sort of a disease?"

The Coast Guard Reserve

In those days, there was a military draft. My friends were drafted into the army. I received a letter with a one-way subway ticket and was ordered to report to Whitehall Street for military duty in the army. That same day, I was admitted to the Coast Guard Reserve. I chose the Coast Guard Reserve, and was sent away from Pat and my family to Cape May, New Jersey, for six weeks of basic training.

The Coast Guard was an adventure. Our company (R-23) consisted of men from a variety of professions, including young men who wanted to be lifelong Coast Guardsmen. I was categorized as a science teacher, since I had done high school science teaching. The first thing the chief said to us in a deep Texas drawl was, "Which of you boys is Jewish?" Several of us looked at each other without saying anything. Then someone reluctantly raised his hand, and all the other Jewish boys did the same, including me. "Get dressed. You boys is going to church," the chief announced. We were driven to a synagogue where there was a religious service, food, and even girls to talk to. This became a regular feature of our Coast Guard "training" thereafter.

The chief knew that I was a teacher and he appointed me as company yeoman. The yeoman was the only person permitted to leave the base to buy things for the others, so I became well liked by all. Then the recruit company commander was assaulted by some of the other recruits. The chief approached me and said, "How would you like to be company commander, Druger?"

I did some quick thinking. "I like being yeoman, sir, but I'll do it if I can keep both jobs." The chief agreed, so I was company commander and yeoman at the same time.

One of my memorable moments as company commander was when a high-level Coast Guard official visited the base. I was ordered to be the second battalion commander for the day. The troops were standing with rifles at their side, waiting for the command to lift the rifle to their shoulder. The regimental commander issued the command. The first battalion commander repeated the order to lift their rifles and I was supposed to repeat that command to my battalion.

"Attention!" yelled the regimental commander.

"Attention," echoed the first battalion commander.

I passed on this command to my troops: "Attention!"

Then the regimental commander yelled, "Right shoulder." The first battalion commander yelled, "Right shoulder." I turned my head and yelled to my battalion, "Forward." The men in my battalion started marching aimlessly around, dragging their rifles. I was embarrassed, but I was not dismissed as company commander.

Another memorable incident involved the raising of the American flag. Each day, the base commander would watch this event from his barrack's window. He considered this to be a sacred event. I led the honor guard of four men to raise the flag. We marched to the flagpole under my direction. There was a maze of pathways and there was another flagpole at the other side of the maze. Under the patriotic gaze of the base commander and an entire regiment of Coast Guardsmen, I marched the honor guard to the wrong flagpole. "Whoops . . . about face!" Again, the incident did not cost me my company commander job.

As company commander, I gave my friends the easy jobs, for example, sorting mail or dusting the barracks, while I assigned other recruits to cleaning latrines.

One day, our company was marching toward another company. When both met, there was shoving and pushing. I commanded the troops to halt, and then yelled at them. "This is not the Boy Scouts," I said, "this is the Coast Guard. The next person that gets out of line will get two hours of extra duty." This meant the person would have to carry a rifle and a full backpack and march around at night in the freezing cold.

"Except for your friends," someone shouted.

I pointed my finger at that voice and said, "And you're the first one to get extra duty . . . and your friend next to you." I'm sure my finger shook as I realized whom I was pointing at. They were the two men who had assaulted the former company commander.

As we marched back to the barracks, I had strong misgivings about my threat. But as a teacher, I knew that, if you make a threat, you must carry it out. As the two men exited the barracks for extra duty that night, they said, "We'll get you, Druger."

In a shaky voice, I said, "You deserved it."

The professionals in the company only had three months of basic training, while the regulars had six months. So the professionals left the company sooner than the others. The night before we left, the regulars were going to "get me." My friends circled my bed to protect me. I later discovered that the two men I had assigned extra duty did not go along with this plan. I always have felt that this was because they respected the fact that I had the courage to carry out my threat in spite of potentially severe consequences. The lesson: If you make a threat, be prepared to carry it out.

Several months after basic training was finished, Pat and I returned to our apartment from an evening out. There was a napkin taped to the door. Scrawled in red was the message, "We were here, you weren't. We'll be back."

I told Pat about my threatening incident in the Coast Guard, and gave her the names of the two men. "If anything happens to me," I said, "you know who did it."

It turned out that my brother and sister-in-law paid us a surprise visit, and we weren't home. So she wrote a message on a napkin in red lipstick and taped it to the door. Whew!

3 Misadventures in Teaching

I started teaching science as a student teacher at Midwood High School in Brooklyn in 1954. It's hard to believe that I have been teaching for so long, so I recently sent for my transcript. It was true. I had grown old very fast.

Teaching a large introductory college biology course was my specialty for more than fifty years. This course enrolled many hundreds of students, and I estimate that I've taught more than 40,000 students in my teaching career. Everyone asks what changes I've observed in first-year college students over the years. Basically, I think students are more knowledgeable about world affairs, more serious about their career goals, more self-centered, and more technologically oriented, and there is great variation in maturity. One mature student said to me, "My father is sacrificing a lot for me to be here, and I'm not going to let him down." A typical comment from an immature student is, "Do we have to know that? Is that on the exam?" Some students "get it," while others don't "get it" . . . yet. The immature students may get it in five years, ten years, or twenty years, but not now.

Technology

A major factor is technology. I grew up with radio. I regularly listened to *The Lone Ranger, The Shadow, Lorenzo Jones, Superman,* and other classic programs. I actually had to use my imagination. Then television arrived and nothing was left to the imagination. The early TV sets had a tiny screen in a huge box. The image was black and white. Soon, advances in technology revolutionized the world. Now you can watch bigger-than-life football games in living color on TV, where you think you've scored the touchdown yourself. Computers have replaced typewriters, and we can find out facts about any topic using the World Wide Web. Most students have an iPod glued to their ears or are talking or text messaging on a cell phone.

One day, I spotted a male student on campus walking around in circles and talking to himself. I thought he was having a mental problem, so I approached him to help. When I got closer, I saw that he had some device in his ear—one of the newfangled cell phones—and he was talking to his friend.

Eventually, technology will find a way to implant iPods into the brain. As a consequence of text messaging, I predict that students will not be able to spell real words. "ICU" is good enough for effective communication. Nobody can be alone for an instant. I wrote a poem about this modern phenomenon:

Being Alone

I sat alone one day
And watched the people walking,
They had iPods in their ears,
Or were on their cell phones, talking.

I thought how nice it was
To be sitting all alone,
And watch nature all around me,
And not be on the phone.

A squirrel darted by,
And I watched a honeybee,
I saw flowers show their colors,
And green leaves dressed up the tree.

It was a cloudy day,
But the temperature was warm,
I felt the breeze and wondered
If there'd be a thunderstorm.

I sat there all alone,
While I heard their cell phones ringing,
They had iPods in their ears,
While I heard robins singing.

All students seem to know all about the latest tech-nology. I asked my young grandson to teach me how to use some software on the computer. He told me, "I'm too advanced to teach you that." Now, I have learned that when I run into a computer problem, I can solve it very easily. Pat has a master's degree in mathematics from Syracuse University and is proficient in computer use. I simply yell, "Pat . . . help!"

One day, the alarm on my watch went off while I was lecturing on the auditorium stage. I didn't know what to do. I had one of those cheap watches that require that you push button 1 twice, then push button 2, then push both together, and so on. A student calmly came to the stage from the audience and said, "I'll fix it," and he did.

Pat and I differ on how to find directions when we are lost somewhere. Pat turns to maps. I ask the first person we see on the street for directions. I told a six-year-old girl about our different approaches, and I asked, "If you were lost, how would you find directions?" She replied, "GPS."

The good news is that students know the technology; the bad news is that they use it endlessly.

The Hiring

When I returned to the United States after a postdoctoral research fellowship at the Commonwealth Scientific and Industrial Research Organization (CSIRO) in Sydney, Australia, I was offered two jobs. One was at the University of Michigan; the other was at Syracuse University. My family lived in the Northeast, and I was inclined towards the Syracuse job.

I was teaching a laboratory class of high school students that summer at Syracuse University. The department chair that was considering hiring me brought the vice chancellor into the lab to meet me. The chair said, "Marv, I'd like you to meet the vice chancellor."

I said, "Hi. Nice to meet you. Please excuse me; I'm teaching a class." And I went back to the students. The vice chancellor looked stunned, and he left.

I guess he was impressed by my dedication to the students . . . or by my boldness. I was hired at Syracuse University.

Our Mission as Teachers

I was driving my car thinking about what education is all about. Then I had an epiphany. *Our mission as teachers is to provide meaningful, motivational experiences that enrich the lives of students and help them identify their unique talents and where they fit in life.*

Students memorize information for exams and then forget much of the information right after the exam. But they don't forget *experiences*. Experiences make them think about life in a new way, and even the most trivial experience can stay with them. My philosophy is that *we learn from everything that we do, and everything that we do becomes part of what we are.*

So I am adamant about enforcing experiences and attendance. If you don't attend the experiences of a course, you miss them, and nobody can adequately explain what you've missed. You'll never know what experience might change your entire life.

I told my students how important it was to attend every class, for the experience as well as the information. One student remarked, "But if I'm experiencing your class, I'm missing another experience."

My years of experience enabled me to respond, "Yes, but you have to set priorities. If the other experience is doing the laundry, then you have to make a choice."

My course policy was to give students an F in the course for lack of attendance, regardless of grades on exams. In my older years, I softened, and merely lowered the grade significantly for lack of attendance.

Students were afraid to miss my lectures. They sent memorable emails:

> I am writing to let you know that I will not be in class on April 23. I am stranded at home because Logan Airport has suffered severe radar failure. (*Actually, regular radar failure would have been sufficient as an excuse.*)

> I would like to apologize for missing your Bio 121 lecture today. Finally, the rigors of hard work and long nights got the better of me and I slept through your class. I should note that I was happily dreaming of the wonderful world of biology while I engaged in my irresponsible slumber.

> I'm mailing you concerning my absence from your lecture this morning (10:40 A.M.). I had no intention of

missing this class but I honestly believe that the situation was out of my control. I'll try to make this short, and I hope you understand.

Last weekend, I traveled back home to Texas to visit my family and friends, and watch my little brother play football. Upon trying to return to Syracuse, I encountered numerous problems. My flight was to leave Dallas/Fort Worth airport at 3:00 P.M., en route to Cincinnati, Ohio. Unfortunately, the plane didn't arrive in Dallas until 3:45 P.M. Therefore, I was unable to catch my connecting flight out of Cincinnati, and I was stranded at the Cincinnati airport. Realizing that I had two classes this morning, I made every attempt to return to Syracuse by 8:00 A.M. Because there was no other flight to Syracuse out of Cincinnati until late Monday afternoon, I decided to fly to New York City, where I could catch an early flight (6:00 A.M.) to Syracuse the following morning. Adding to the drama, my flight out of Cincinnati, which was scheduled to take off at 10:45, had mechanical problems. I eventually reached NYC at 2:30 A.M. Monday morning. I was reserved a hotel room by the airline, and I eventually saw my room at about 3:30 A.M. I saw no point in going to bed. Besides, I probably wouldn't wake up if I did. I arranged for a wake-up call at 5:00 A.M., and even set an alarm anyway. Unfortunately, I was unable to stay awake and the wake-up calls had no effect on me. I awoke at 8:00 A.M. and took the next flight to Syracuse (11:10 A.M.). . . . Well, that is how I have spent the last 24 hours. I apologize for missing your lecture. I hope to obtain the information covered from a classmate. Thank you for your time, and have a good evening.

This is what I call a conscientious student.

Oftentimes, non-science-major seniors were the ones who slacked off on attendance. I told one such senior that his lack of attendance would result in an F in the course. He responded, "You can't do that to me. I'm a senior."

"You're doing it to yourself," I said. "You know the course policy. It's stated on the second page of the syllabus."

"I never turned the page," he said.

I had him assist me in teaching a small class of students. He made up the missed quizzes and earned a B+ in the course, and had a very valuable experience in life.

The Phone Calls

At midterm one semester I noticed that a number of students were not attending class regularly. I decided to phone each student. I would start with, "Hello. This is Dr. Druger. I've noticed that you have not been attending class regularly, and I just want to check on your health. Are you okay?" The first response was usually, "I've been there. I just forgot to sign an attendance sheet." After our phone conversation, the student's final comment was often, "I'm sorry. I'll be there from now on. Thanks for calling."

During one phone call to a delinquent student, I said, "I like your attitude. From now on, why don't you come up to me after lecture and say hello?" Sure enough, that student would come up to me after lecture: "Hi, I'm here."

I think students who were called appreciated being reminded about the importance of experiences in life. One note said, "You caught me off guard with your phone call. I didn't expect a professor to call my house. I'm surprised that you took the time and effort to do that. Not many, or any of the professors I know would have taken the interest or the time to do so. That is something I admire. I have been told that students are just a number once we reach college, but you have showed me that you do not think along those lines. . . . I will be in lecture next week at the front of the class. Thank you once again."

Student Behavior in the Large Lecture Class

Although most students were attentive in my large lecture class, some students spent time talking to their neighbor, text messaging, talking on cell phones, watching movies, sleeping, or playing games on their laptop computers. Occasionally, students entered the classroom late or left early. I was told that this was not uncommon behavior in large lecture classes. I decided to wage a campaign to bring better decorum to the lecture hall.

One day, during my lecture, a young man stood up, waved to his girlfriend next to him, and both of them arrogantly walked toward the exit in the back of the auditorium with a swagger in their step. I got angry. I jumped off the auditorium stage and ran up the center aisle to catch them. I accosted them outside the door.

"Your parents are paying a lot for this course. If you stayed, you might learn something," I scolded. One of the students came back into the auditorium, and the other one left. When I returned to the platform, the room was totally silent. I had the portable microphone switched on, and everyone had heard me yelling at the two students. That incident cured the "leave early" problem. From then on, students were afraid to get up and leave.

Another day, a young man sheepishly got up and walked toward the back of the auditorium. I wasn't going to say anything, but when he reached the door, he stopped, and with his face red, he turned and said, "I really gotta go." He returned a few minutes later. I guess if you gotta go, you gotta go.

Once each semester, I deliberately planned to run after students who left class suspiciously. I spotted a young man and woman rise from their seats and swagger toward the exit. "Ah ha, this is it!" I jumped off the auditorium stage and raced to the back of the auditorium to catch them. When I got to the door, they were running down the street. They successfully escaped.

Sometimes, I could tell if a student really had to "go." As a student walked up the aisle of the auditorium toward the door, I stopped in the middle of my sentence and stared at him for a moment or two. The class was in a state of suspense. Will he do it, or not? And then I simply went on with the lecture as though nothing had happened. Whew!

Misadventures in Teaching

Once a student was obviously reading a book in the last row of the lecture hall. I stopped in the middle of my lecture and said, "That young man who's reading a book back there. Will you please hold up the book? I'd like to see what book is more interesting than my lecture." The student who I'd seen reading didn't move, but another student about ten rows in front of him held up a book. I wasn't even talking to him. I'll bet that if I made my comment to the class as a whole, many students would have held up the books they were reading. I didn't try it.

The next week, while giving a lecture, I noticed a young lady in the middle of the lecture hall typing furiously on her red laptop computer. She didn't look up at me, and I suspected that she was text messaging or playing computer games. I jumped off the stage and ran to her seat.

"What are you doing?" I asked accusingly. "Are you text messaging or playing games?"

She looked at me and said, "I'm taking notes." And, indeed, she was taking notes.

I was embarrassed. I said, "You are a great student. Your parents should be proud of you." I later sent her an email with my apologies for being so suspicious.

One student approached me after a lecture and complained about some students near him who were chatting inappropriately during the lecture. He said, "I'm paying thousands of dollars to hear you talk, not to hear them talk."

So I tried two new approaches. The direct approach that appeals to the "adult" in every student works well.

I said to the class, "What do you do when someone in back of you in a movie is talking? You say 'shhhh,' or 'be quiet.' What do you do when someone is talking near you in lecture? Nothing. You're paying about $8.50 for the movie, while you're paying more than $85 for the lecture." After this remark, the class became quiet and I started hearing "shhhh."

I also assigned students in a supplementary class to sit in different parts of the auditorium and record the behavior of students around them. Inappropriate behavior was evident. I sent each student in the large class an email on how disappointed I was in their behavior, pointing out that it showed lack of consideration for the professor and for their fellow students. After that communication, there was complete silence during future lectures, except for questions. Do you know how quiet quiet is? It was so quiet that I sometimes forgot what I was talking about.

The moral of these stories is that students do not misbehave with malicious intent. They were not out to "get me." They were simply thoughtless, inconsiderate, or rude. Once inappropriate behavior and its implications were brought to their attention in a direct way, they responded positively. "I never thought about it that way before" is a key to learning and changing behavior. If students would leave each class with at least one new idea that they "never thought about that way before," they would end up with a good education.

Some Exam Reforms

I arranged three major exams in the fall semester and three in the spring semester. I tried to remedy some of the faults that I perceived in exams when I was a student. My exams were given in the evening and students had two hours or more to complete a one-hour exam. I wanted to know how well the students knew the content, not how fast they knew it. This flexibility in time eliminated the nauseous stomach syndrome that students get when the teacher says, "You have only a few minutes left."

Because of the large class size, the major exams were multiple choice, but essay quizzes were given by teaching assistants. Old exams were available in the library as samples. My exams usually involved modifying old questions on the same content. For example, an old exam would ask about blood typing where a father was type A and a mother was type B. I would alter this question so that the father was type AB and the mother type A. If the students understood blood typing, they would choose the correct answer no matter what the types I used in the question. Sample exam questions were also included in the laboratory guide. The goal was that there were no surprises, and students knew the types of questions that would be asked. The philosophy was that if I know what I think is important for the students to know, then why not tell them? Why should students have to guess about what my experience says is important?

Exams also had humorous covers. The students could laugh at the cover and reduce anxiety before tackling the exam questions.

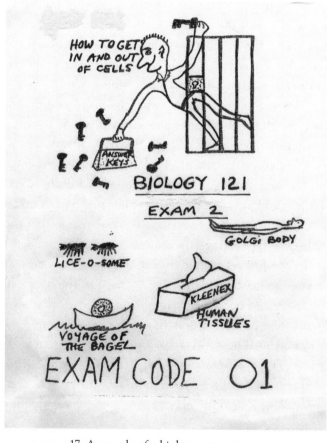

17. A sample of a biology exam cover.

Throwing Answer Keys Out of the Window—The Druger Drop

When I gave major exams, I used many rooms on campus. I thought it was important for students to find out answers and their scores immediately after the exam, so that they could learn while they were especially interested. As students left their exam room, they were given an answer key. Then I discovered several cheating incidents. A student would leave the room with an answer key, come back under the pretense of leaving something behind, and drop the answer key on a friend's desk.

The most bizarre case of cheating happened on a cold, snowy day. Students were seated a seat apart and one young man sat near a partially open window. The student sitting near him said, "Will you please close the window, I'm freezing."

The young man responded, "I have asthma and I need the air." When the exam proctor stepped out of the room for a moment, a paper airplane came flying through the window from outside. It was an answer key that someone had picked up in another exam room. "You see why I wanted the window open," the young man said. It turned out that the other student's father was a professor in the Forestry College, and she reported the incident. An investigation revealed that the student was getting $1 deposit and $4 on delivery of answer keys to students in different rooms. The deliveryman was punished for his misdeeds.

Because of the cheating incidents, I sought another way of distributing answers to students immediately after the exams. I told students that I would personally give out the answer keys at a designated time after the exam. The biology office was on the third floor of a building. At 9:00 P.M., I tried to walk down the stairs from the third floor. The stairwell was packed with students and I couldn't make any progress. So I went to the window and threw out one answer key. Someone yelled, "He's throwing them out the window." The students emptied out the hallway, and I walked downstairs and gave out the answer keys. That was the beginning of a long tradition of throwing answer keys out the window after exams.

Then the groundskeepers planted a tree and put a giant rock on the lawn under the third floor window. I went to class and announced, "They landscaped the area on the street under the window. I won't throw the answer keys out the window tonight. I'm afraid someone will get hurt."

My announcement was met with groans of "Ahhhhh . . . Let's do it."

"Okay," I said, "I'll throw out the answer keys tonight."

Students were gathered on the street under the window, yelling "Jump! Jump!" Just before I was about to throw the answer keys out of the window, a paper airplane floated down from the fourth floor window above. There was a brief scuffle in the street below. The next thing I knew, there was an ambulance on the street. The attendants picked up a body and drove off.

18. Marvin tossing answer keys to the biology exam from a second-floor window in Lyman Hall to the frenzied crowd below. Many of the answer keys were autographed, wishing students a happy bio-life. Photo by Steve Sartori.

Later that night, students called me at home: "Some-one was killed!" "Someone was broke her leg." "Someone was badly hurt."

I later discovered that a young lady was standing on the large rock and was unprepared for my paper toss. When the paper floated down from the window above, there was a scuffle and she slipped off the rock and sprained her ankle. Incidentally, I'm sure that a student whom I know, but never have seen since, tossed the paper out of the fourth floor window as a practical joke.

Weeks later, I was told that there was a meeting of university administrators. Someone asked, "What profes-sor throws answer keys out the window?"

"Oh, that's Druger," someone answered. There was silence, and they moved on to another topic.

I didn't want anyone to be injured because of the "Druger Drop," so I decided to discontinue this practice. Now the challenge was to find a new way to distribute answer keys after the exams. A student suggested that I do a program on the student TV station that reached all the residence halls. Thus the one-hour *Bio-Answer Show* was conceived. I made up a humorous skit to start the show. After the skit, I went over the answers to the test. Then I had a lottery at the end of the show. Every stu-dent's name was in a fishbowl. With the help of a student, I randomly picked winners of Dollar Store prizes. The show was done in a humorous, professional manner and was a big success.

The show had a studio audience of about twenty-five students. Once, only one student showed up. Whenever I said something special, he would clap slowly and deliberately. He was on TV and was the star of the show.

Then, during one *Bio-Answer Show,* disaster struck. We received phone calls at the studio that no one could tune in the show. I was told that there was some construction, and the cables from the studio were accidentally cut. The broadcast was going nowhere. It was time to get back to throwing answer keys out the window, and this was the way answer keys were given out since then.

I tried to improve the Druger Drop and make it more exciting for the students. By then, a student had filmed the event, and it was on YouTube. I labeled twenty-five answer keys and wrote, "Congratulations! You have just won two extra points on the exam. Bring this paper to the biology office and your two points will be recorded." This procedure created a mad frenzy among the students when the answers were tossed out the window: "I was shoved ten feet away from where I was standing." "I was thrown over someone's back." "Someone knocked me down and stepped on my face." One student rushed into my office with a crumpled half of an answer key page and asked, "Can I get one point?" When I drove home later that night, I saw four students wistfully staring at an answer key that was stuck at the top of a tall tree, trying to figure out how to reach it. I later found out that they did get that answer key by throwing a basketball at it. How clever! To avoid any student injuries in the future, I eliminated the extra-two-pointers from future drops.

P-P-P-E-P: The Art of Teaching

I teamed up with an undergraduate to create a twenty-minute film on important aspects of teaching, that is, preparation, presentation, people-orientation, evaluation, and practice (hence P-P-P-E-P). I assembled an all-star cast of graduate and undergraduate students. One actor who played the part of a teaching assistant in the film had done beer commercials in Hollywood. The student class was supposed to be honors students, but they failed to show up for the filming. I phoned my daughter who was a student at Syracuse University and she rounded up her friends, who did a superb job of acting. I played the part of the guiding spirit who analyzed and discussed teaching scenes. I dressed in cap and gown and rode a mule that I paid $50 to rent. Martha was superb and didn't poop once on the campus.

Druger's Zoo

I had a radio interview program on WAER (88.3 FM) for about thirteen years. The program, called *Druger's Zoo*, featured random human beings who happened to walk by the studio. I recorded five five-minute programs in one day, and one was played each day Monday through Friday. The interviews were generally with non-famous, everyday people who talked about their lives and jobs.

19. Marvin riding a mule on campus as part of his teaching assistant training film: "P-P-P-E-P: The Art of Teaching." Photo by Steve Sartori.

The most famous person I interviewed was Famous Amos, the cookie man. He happened to be walking past the studio. I called to him from a window and asked him if I could interview him for the radio program. He agreed.

I asked him, "What made you so famous, Famous?" "Confidence, man, confidence," was his reply. He exuded confidence.

"What do you do differently now that you are so rich and famous, Famous?" I asked. "I have a house in Hawaii, but if you have two houses you can only live in one. I have two cars, but you can only drive one. What more is there than what you need?" A wise remark from a successful, wise man. "What more is there than what you need?"

I almost missed a program only once in all those years. My guest didn't show up. So I faked an international accent, and interviewed myself as Dr. Nivram Regurd (Marvin Druger backward). Because I was in disguise, I felt free to be more flamboyant than I otherwise would be. I was more interesting than the real me.

Druger's Australian Zoo

While visiting western Australia, I did a radio interview program on 6NR in Perth. This was a thirty-minute program that revealed the lifestyles of regular people in different occupations. The program started with a musical burst of "Yankee Doodle Dandy."

En route to western Australia by train, we stopped at a small town that consisted of a pub and a few houses.

I interviewed the bartender. "This is a small, isolated town. What do you do for excitement?" I asked. The bartender replied, "Darts." He told me that wife swapping was another favorite activity.

Druger's Washington Zoo

While serving as a program officer at the National Science Foundation in Washington, D.C., I taped interviews with Washington dignitaries and sent the tapes to WAER in Syracuse to be aired. I had heard about all the wonderful cocktail parties in Washington, D.C., but Pat and I were never invited to any. So we decided to have a cocktail party in our apartment. The invitation said that the party was from 5:00 to 8:00 P.M. At 8:00, the party was at its peak. Conversation was flowing and everyone was happy. Then a guest accidentally leaned on the light switch. The lights blinked. Everyone looked at their watches, noted the time, and suddenly left. The light flicker was the end to what could have been a long, delightful evening.

Druger's Working World

Another venture into educational media was a television program on a local television station in Syracuse. The purpose of *Druger's Working World* was to explore different occupations for high school and college students. I made nine thirty-minute, on-site interview programs that featured individuals in different occupations and what their jobs were all about. For example, I did one on law enforcement. In this program, I rode in a police helicopter, was in a jail cell, and was attacked by Shamos, the German shepherd police dog. They put a padded sleeve on my arm and told me to start running away. At the command of the dog trainer, Shamos galloped after me and clamped its teeth on my arm. I yelled at him, but he would only respond to the command of his trainer. I remember this terrifying event every time I see a dog.

Another program was about occupations in finance. I started the program dressed in old jeans and a torn shirt. I ate a rotten banana that I found in a garbage can. Then I went to a pawnbroker and offered to sell him a copy of a *Druger's Working World* tape. "That's worthless," he said. "If you need money, then you'd better go to the credit union." So I interviewed the agent at the credit union. Each time that I moved to a different person in finances, I dressed more elegantly. For the last interview, a former student who worked for a limousine company drove me up to an elegant home in Syracuse. I got out of the limo dressed in a tuxedo and I interviewed the president of Onondaga Bank, who was waiting for me outside the house.

These programs were popular, and the TV station played the series over and over again.

Science on the Radio

A number of years after *Druger's Zoo* ended, I decided to pursue my radio hobby once again. This time, the program was a ninety-second segment that I named *Science on the Radio*. The series was aired on WAER at 10:30 A.M. and 2:30 P.M. on Tuesdays and Thursdays. The programs were intended to enhance the scientific literacy of the general public. How does a ballpoint pen work? How does a refrigerator work? What is superconductivity? How does a curveball curve? How does an insect fly? What's going on in space exploration? Eventually, the program became known in the Syracuse community, and some people told me that they listened regularly. I didn't listen regularly to the program myself. I learned a lot from researching the topics, and I had excellent student producers working with me.

I particularly like being on the radio because the audience can't see you. You may grow older, but your voice doesn't. Television reveals the progression of wrinkles and gray hair and worse. So I'll stay with radio as long as I can.

The Bio-Creativity Project

I wanted to encourage students to use their creativity, so I initiated the Bio-Creativity Project as an optional experience. The assignment was to create something about *life*. The prize was a poster-sized, autographed copy of the photo of me in academic robes riding a mule. Very few students did projects. Why would they want that prize?

I thought of a better idea; that is, add some points to their grade. Then hundreds of students did projects. The creativity of students was impressive. With permission, I kept projects that I particularly liked. One project was a pair of white sneakers adorned with butterflies with the inscription "Shoes of Life." Another project was a microscope made out of hard candies. Another project was a lamp with my caricature face carved into the lampshade, so that my face would glow when the light was on. Two huge football players brought me their project. They baked a cake with a diagram of cell components in the frosting. Another student glued garbage found in the residence hall into the shape of a pig. A great variety of poems, songs, essays, and posters were created. One student came to my office to sing the song she had written about biology.

I learned that students could be very creative. Just ask them to use their creativity.

Words of Wisdom

Sometimes students made memorable comments. One student was getting a prestigious award for his research project. He was obviously nervous when he had to say a few words to acknowledge the award. He stepped to the microphone and briefly summarized his project. His final words were, "I learned that anything can be impossible."

Benefit-of-the-Doubt Credit

Some students complained that there was nothing to do on campus. The complaint was usually because they weren't doing anything. There were always worthwhile activities available for students.

I organized extra evening lectures by scientists as optional enrichments for students. Students obtained a ticket and turned it in after the lectures. We kept a record of attendance and, at grading time, if they attended a reasonable number of these extra sessions, students were given benefit-of-the-doubt credit. This credit would help if their grade was on the borderline at the end of the semester. Students would do almost anything for benefit-of-the-doubt credit, and hundreds of students attended the extracurricular sessions.

Too Much Lecturing

Modern pedagogy emphasizes inquiry, discussion, critical thinking, and active involvement of students in the learning process. I believe in the effectiveness of these approaches to teaching, but I rely heavily on lecturing. A past chancellor of the university agreed to give a lecture to my class. He started by saying, "I'm glad that Marv's here to substitute for me, if I didn't get here on time. Actually, Marv's a better speaker, but you'd be here longer."

One hot, sultry August day, I lectured to a class of prospective college science teachers. The class was three hours long. As I talked, students were sweating from the heat and they were squirming uncomfortably in their chairs.

"Can we take a break?" one student asked.

"Sure," I replied, "As soon as I finish this next point." I never did finish that point, and the students had to endure three hours of lecturing under very uncomfortable conditions.

I remedied the situation the next class meeting. "Do you remember how uncomfortable it was to sit through a three-hour lecture in the steaming heat? I did that deliberately to show you what it would feel like. As a teacher, you should never do that." My excuse seemed to work well.

Students became used to my tendency to talk too much. My typical approach in class was to say, "Today we're going to have a discussion," and then I would lecture until the class ended.

One student wrote this comment: "I don't learn nothing in lecture." I took that as a compliment. If he didn't learn nothing, then he must have learned something.

I taught a weekly seminar for my graduate students. This seminar was intended to exchange and discuss research ideas in science education. I dominated the sessions with my lectures. Then the students started bringing food to share at the seminar. There was a lot more active discussion, and I lectured much less. One of the students revealed the class's psychology. She announced, "A full mouth is a quiet mouth." The approach worked.

Actually, lecturing fits my philosophy about teaching. Teachers should be prepared to use all teaching strategies, but they should also be aware of which ones they do best, and not feel obliged to use an approach because it's "supposed" to be best. I'd rather have a great lecture from a teacher who lectures well, than have a poor inquiry lesson from that person who doesn't do inquiry lessons very well. It all depends.

Midnight Lectures

Some students complained that they could not attend extra evening lectures because they had to work when these lectures were scheduled. "Do you work at midnight?" I asked. "Well, not exactly." "Great, then you can attend the lectures at midnight."

The midnight lecture featured a researcher and, at first, was from 11:00 P.M. to midnight. At midnight, I would draw tickets from a fishbowl and award Dollar Store door prizes.

As I grew older, I couldn't stay up until midnight, so the midnight lectures were given at 8:00 or 9:00 P.M.

My Son, the Doctor

I recruited my ophthalmologist son to give a midnight lecture on vision. During the lecture, he mistakenly tried to use the laser pointer to advance the slides instead of using the remote control device. I tried to reassure him by yelling out, "That's okay. I do that all the time." He responded, "Yes, but you keep doing it for ten minutes . . . and then call Mom to ask her why it doesn't work."

A student asked my son if his dad was like this at home also. My son replied, "He's exactly the same. He drives my mom crazy."

My son occasionally appeared on a radio call-in show. I decided to call in a question: "Bob, you said that my cataracts would be very difficult to do surgery on. Why would my surgery be so difficult, and for people like me?"

My son replied, "In your case, it would be difficult to keep you lying down and quiet."

Impregnation

I gave a presentation to the new teaching assistants at Syracuse University. As chair of the Department of Science Teaching, I complained about the difficulties of being chair of a department. "The chair is blamed for whatever happens," I said. "If someone breaks the window, it's the chair's fault. If someone puts chewing gum in the door lock, it's the chair's fault." A random thought suddenly emerged from my mouth: "If the secretary becomes pregnant, it's the chair's fault." This spontaneous, stupid remark evoked some subdued laughter.

After the lecture, an international teaching assistant confronted me and said, "What you said was terrible. You said that you impregnated the secretary." I tried to explain that my remark was a joke, and that I really didn't impregnate the secretary. But the young lady was offended, and she angrily walked away. This is another example of why words need to be processed in your brain before they leave your mouth.

My Best Lectures

Most teachers would like students in their lecture to be thinking, captivated, and excited. The audience at a

Sunday sermon on TV has glowing faces, intent concentration, and an eagerness to hear the words of the minister. Sometimes that happens in class. But most of the time it does not. The students sit passively, daring the teacher to excite or motivate them to learn.

A few years ago, for my last lecture of the semester, I dressed like the modern human. I had a cap on backwards, earrings, sunglasses, fake tattoos on my arms, a backpack, a Marv Druger fan club T-shirt, baggy jeans, sneakers, a cell phone, and a water bottle. I appeared in class without any explanation and gave a regular lecture. Students were fascinated. Their eyes and ears were glued to my presentation. In the middle of the lecture, I deliberately tripped and fell to the floor, but still had my cell phone near my ear. This was a very successful lecture. I had their full attention. I was one of them.

Another time, I had a terrible case of the flu. Nevertheless, I showed up to give my lecture. I was nauseous, sweaty, pale green, and could barely speak into the microphone. I gave a regular lecture. Once in a while, I would stop and slowly go over to a table where there was a water bottle. As I sipped the water, I could read the minds of the students, "Is he okay? Will he die?" I certainly had their full attention.

Sometimes lectures bomb completely, despite thorough preparation. An experienced teacher senses when this is happening. Sometimes I would simply forget what I was talking about. Sometimes I would put myself to sleep with my own lecture. Other times, I would get myself

20. Marvin lecturing to 350 students while dressed like a "modern human," including earrings, a cap on backwards, a backpack, tattoos, sunglasses, sneakers, a Marvin Druger fan club T-shirt, and baggy jeans. Of course, he also had a cell phone and a bottle of water. Photo by Steve Sartori.

confused as I tried to explain a complex concept. Sometimes I would simply stop in the middle of the lecture and say to myself, "What the hell am I talking about?" But it all seemed to come out well at the end. Most of the time, my "terrible lecture" that created posttraumatic stress in me was accepted by students. "What's the big deal?"

It was reassuring to realize that teachers can expect bad days when nothing works well. It may be the weather, your mood, the content, the students' mood, or any number of incidental factors. The best we can do is to expect things not to go well all the time. Failure is part of life, and our sense of failure is often not recognized as such by students.

I remember giving a good, content-oriented lecture to high school students. Pat was with me in the classroom. After the lecture, I said to Pat, "See, I know more than you think."

She replied, "You hide it very well."

Students often do appreciate a good lecture. After one of my marathon lectures, I apologetically remarked to a student in the class, "I'm sorry, but I talk too much."

The student responded, "But you have a lot to say." This was undoubtedly an "A" student.

I gave a lecture just before I was scheduled to have surgery. After class, I said to a student, "I hope that wasn't my last lecture." She commented, "If it was, it was a good one."

Self-awareness is an important part of teaching. We need to recognize our strengths and weaknesses and then

21. The "real" Marvin giving a presentation to elementary school students from H. W. Smith School in Syracuse. Photo by Steve Sartori.

decide what approaches fit us best. Videotaping of our lessons, self-analysis, and peer analysis are useful tools for achieving self-awareness. Teachers need to know what they do well and what they need to improve on. Then translate these findings into classroom action, and students will learn.

Teaching at the Prison

Years ago, Syracuse University offered a special program of courses to enable prisoners at the Auburn Correctional Facility in New York to earn an undergraduate degree. I taught an introductory college biology course at the prison. Once I passed through security, there were classrooms and it almost looked like an ordinary school setting. This is a maximum-security prison, yet the inmates seemed like nice guys to me. It was not proper etiquette to talk about the crimes inmates committed. Yet when I mentioned the subject, it seemed that everyone was innocent. "He slipped and hit his head on the edge of the table. I never touched him." When I left at the end of the fall semester, I announced, "I'll see you all in the spring." The response was: "Yeah. We're not going anywhere."

I was frightened only once during the semester. I was standing in the corridor, wearing a tie and jacket, when the bell rang to change classes. Inmates rushed past me, going in all directions. I felt very vulnerable; someone could have easily stabbed me in passing and nobody would ever know.

I wanted to have the inmates dissect a fetal pig as part of the biology course. I discussed this project with the warden. "We'll need scalpels," I said, "but I'll make sure that I get all of them back after the dissection."

The warden laughed, "Yes, you'll get the scalpels in your back. There are too many weapons in the yard now. We don't need any more." My naïveté was obvious. There was no dissection, after all.

Greeting the President

A few years ago, former president Bill Clinton was the speaker at commencement. Pat and I served as marshalls. We were told not to shake hands with Clinton, since he likes to shake hands and he would be delayed walking to the platform if he got started. As he passed by, I instinctively put out my hand to shake. The SU photographer (who takes countless photos of Pat and me) snapped a photo just as our hands met for a second. The photo makes us look like best friends. Pat is just across the aisle from us, smiling. She said that her fate in life is to be left out, or to be known as Lauren's, Bob's, or James's mother or Marvin's wife. She does all the work, but doesn't seek the glory.

Big College Versus Small College

Choosing a college is a major decision for students and parents. My son, the ophthalmologist, and my daughter, the

22. Marvin shaking hands with former president Bill Clinton, during the procession of guests at a Syracuse University commencement. Notice Pat's head on the opposite side of the aisle from Bill and Marvin. Photo by Steve Sartori.

former dietitian, now a second-grade teacher, attended Syracuse University. My other son, the businessman, attended a small college. Because of a tuition exchange program for faculty and staff, they all received free tuition. My experiences with a large and a small college lead to the following advice: Students have to choose the college that fits their personality best. After a month in a small school, you know everyone and everyone knows you. At a large school, you can meet someone new every day. The small school probably provides more intimacy, and students will get to know the faculty well. To know faculty well at a large school, you have to step out a bit and be more assertive. The large school usually has more resources and more options. Generally, a large school is not really that large. It's like New York City where millions of people work and live each day. But, as in the city, students don't live with millions of people. They live with friends in their classes and in their housing unit.

The college that my younger son attended specialized in engineering. He didn't really want to pursue an engineering career, but he ended up with a degree in mechanical engineering. Then he attended graduate school in business, and went on to become a sales specialist in technical products for a major firm. So students have to find a college where they best fit.

Cockroaches and Colleges

When I was a program officer at the National Science Foundation in Washington, D.C., Pat and I had to rent an apartment. I hated cockroaches, since they were constant companions in apartments where I grew up. I wanted to find a cockroach-free apartment. When I asked the rental agent if one apartment had cockroaches, he exclaimed, "Of course not. We have the exterminator every week." I wondered, "If you don't have cockroaches, then why do you have the exterminator every week?"

Then I discovered the secret to renting a cockroach-free apartment. When we were in the elevator of an apartment house and someone else entered, I would ask, "Do you live here? Do you have any cockroaches?" "None," was the reply in one building. So we rented an apartment in that building for the year, and it turned out to be cockroach free.

So my advice for seeking a college is to visit the school, go on the regular tour led by a gung-ho student, but stop every student you see on campus and ask, "Do you go to this school? How is it?" This will give you a truer picture of the school, and you'll be in a better position to make the decision about attending.

4 Miscellaneous Misadventures

This chapter is designed to be unusual. Typically a chapter has a theme and ideas should flow in a coherent manner. However, this is not the way our minds always work. When we think about our lives, we recall specific, isolated events that appear in our minds in a haphazard fashion. How does the brain recall information, and why is the timing of that recall so unpredictable? This chapter will illustrate the randomized nature of memory. I will tell about whatever experiences come to mind, without thinking about whether or not these experiences relate to each other in an organized way. Your first reaction may be, "How does one experience relate to the next?" Your second reaction may be, "Hey, this is weird. There are no connections between experiences. What a novel way to write a chapter. I like it!"

Who Am I?

After teaching for more than fifty years, I meet former students all over the world. They usually don't run away but stop to chat about the experiences they had in my biology course. Students have told me that their parents, aunts, and uncles had taken my biology course, but no grandparents. Having taught tens of thousands of students over a span of fifty-four years of teaching, I began to get conceited and felt that I was known all over the world.

I was coediting an issue of the *School Science and Mathematics* journal and I needed a reviewer for one of the articles. I didn't know anyone in the area of that particular submission, so I looked in the literature to find a person who had published articles on that subject. I found someone and sent an email to her asking if she would be willing to review the article.

"Sure thing," she replied. "I'm not sure how to ask this, but who are you? And I apologize profusely if I should know that!"

I was humbled and sent her an outline of my life's accomplishments. I told her to stop the first person that went by in the hallway and mention my name. She sent an apology. "I am embarrassed now! You even have your own bookmarks! In my defense, my degree is in oceanography and I've only recently gotten officially into science education. Your name was familiar!"

A Fan in Yellowstone

One of my colleagues was camping in Yellowstone National Park. A man jogged by wearing a "Marv Druger Fan Club" T-shirt. He stopped to chat. My colleague asked him if he was one of my former students. He replied, "No, but I was in the Syracuse University Bookstore, and I saw this T-shirt on sale, so I bought one." The sale was probably the only way they could sell this T-shirt.

The Award Slipup

I was onstage at the awards banquet at a convention of the National Science Teachers Association (NSTA). I was fortunate enough to be receiving the Carleton Award, the highest honor that NSTA gives for national leadership in science education. After being given a plaque (and a check for $5,000), I made a brief thank-you speech at the podium. I said how privileged I was to receive the award and acknowledged those who supported my efforts. Of course, Pat was one of these supporters.

I looked down from the podium to a table in the right corner of the room. I said, "I could not do what I've done without the support of my wife, Pat, who is sitting at that table over there." I looked toward the table lovingly and said, "Pat, I love you."

A voice yelled out from directly in front of me. "I'm over here taking pictures." And there she was, with camera in hand. Whoops!

Presentation in Mexico

As president of NSTA, I was asked to give a keynote presentation at a science education convention in Mexico.

My talk was instantly translated from English into Spanish. The talk seemed to go well. After the talk, I said to the translator, "Pedro, you did a great job. They even laughed at my jokes."

He said, "No. I'm sorry to tell you that they did not laugh at your jokes. When you told a joke, I said, 'The speaker has told a joke, please laugh.'" I think he was joking.

Pedro told me a story about another speaker whose speech he translated to a large audience. The speaker told some inappropriate jokes, so Pedro told his own jokes. Everyone laughed, and the speaker never knew the difference.

Druger Dollars

Several presidents of the United States have had their faces printed on U.S. currency. As president of the National Science Teachers Association, I thought this might be a good idea. I had "One Hundred Druger" bills printed with a caricature of my face on it. The bill had two of my themes printed on it, "You lead the way with NSTA," and "Teach students to want to learn." My contact information was on the front of the bill, and the back had the dates and sites for upcoming conventions. The Druger Dollar also said, "Free Gift . . . Redeemable at the NSTA Science Store." The motive was to get people to hand in the Druger Dollar at the science store and get a small, pocket magnifier as a gift, and purchase some books. These Druger Dollars were distributed in 1994.

23. Druger Dollars were distributed widely at the 1994 convention of the National Science Teachers Association (NSTA) in Philadelphia. Teachers could bring the Druger Dollars to the convention bookstore to receive a small gift . . . and buy lots of books.

Fourteen years later, I attended an NSTA convention in Boston. I stopped a lady at random in the hotel and asked her where the NSTA registration was. She told me and added, "And I still have my Druger Dollar." I still have a few of these myself.

I magnanimously tried to give a Druger Dollar to a ten-year-old boy. He looked at me and said, "It's fake. I don't want it."

A famous scientist gave a presentation at an NSTA meeting. He signed autographs afterward. A little boy who had obtained the scientist's autograph was standing next to me. Lost in my own importance as president of NSTA, I said to the boy, "Would you like my autograph?"

He firmly and emphatically said, "No!" So much for being president.

The Magnifier and the Caricature

For publicity and fun, I thought of distributing magnifiers in a plastic sleeve. The sleeve had a caricature of my face on it and said, "You lead the way with NSTA," along with my contact information. Years later, I had similar magnifier packets made with just my contact information. I gave them to everyone who would take one. I would proudly and generously announce, "Here's a magnifier for you." The response was often, "Thanks, but I already have one." The ultimate conceit was to have my own face on Druger Dollars and to have magnifiers with that same caricature on it.

Pat programmed the caricature of me on her computerized embroidery sewing machine. She could then embroider it on any clothing item. I was pleased when she put the caricature on my handkerchief. A student had it put on his hat. One lady told me that she wanted one put on a pillowcase, so that she could say that she slept with Marvin.

24. Marvin's magnifiers were first distributed in 1994, when Marvin was president of NSTA. His motto on the magnifier jacket was "Enhance Your Vision with NSTA." Since then, the magnifier jacket has been modified to serve as a business card. Thousands of magnifiers have been given away. When Marvin meets people on the street, the first thing they are likely to exclaim is, "No thanks, I already have one."

Incidentally, a student in my class drew the caricature. I approached him and said, "John, why aren't you taking notes?"

He replied, "I'm drawing pictures of you."

"Great," I said. "Can I use it to advertise myself?" He agreed, and the caricature became my personal logo from then on. I didn't modify the caricature when my hair turned gray on the sides. Vanity prevailed.

Bookmarks

I used the caricature to design a variety of bookmarks to distribute for publicity and fun. I wanted to encourage NSTA to use the experience of past NSTA presidents more fully, so I designed a bookmark that promoted the concept of P-P-P ("Perks for Past Presidents"). Another bookmark summarized the cycle of life. The bookmark had a series of the caricature of me that got smaller from the top to the bottom of the bookmark. The label on the top face was "Marvin Druger, Ad Nauseum, Ad Infinitum." The tiny one at the bottom was labeled, "Marvin Who?" I commented to someone that this bookmark showed what happens in life. You are famous, and then you diminish in importance, as you get older, until nobody knows or cares who you are. I was reassured when the person said, "But you can start with the tiny face at the bottom of the bookmark and work your way upward." I never thought of it that way.

The Scroll

The presidents of NSTA had a scroll that they were supposed to write something on. Someone in the group said,

25. The bookmark of sequences in life. The caricature of Marvin's face was drawn by John P. Norton, illustrator and cartoonist. www.john nortonart.com/ (johnart@starpower .net).

"Write something simple." A past president responded, "Yes . . . write Marvin Druger."

The Book Signing

As president of NSTA, I was strolling through the book exhibit at the national convention. I spotted a colleague sitting at a table with a pile of books. A sign said, "Book-signing." I had no idea what "book-signing" meant. As president of NSTA, I went to the table, picked up a book, and, before the author could protest, I signed it. The author looked shocked. NSTA owned those books and she had to buy that copy herself. I apologized for my ignorant act and bought her a present.

The Cardboard Cutout

I had a great idea for the Philadelphia NSTA convention. I had a life-sized cardboard cutout made of me with arms outstretched to greet everyone who entered the convention hall. The sign hanging on it said, "Welcome to the convention." The cutout was a great hit. It looked more like me than I did. People commented, "Oh, there's Marv. Let's go over and say hello." But it wasn't really me (or was it?). Many people took photos with their arm around the cutout. One teacher put her dress over the outstretched arm and took a photo. I walked by when five teachers were standing around the cutout. I heard one teacher say, "Okay, at five o'clock, 113 we meet at Marvin." The cutout added excitement to the convention.

A few weeks after the convention, a giant, door-sized, rectangular package, addressed to Pat, was delivered to my home. It was me.

Eventually, the cutout ended up at the base of a staircase leading to the book section of the Syracuse University Bookstore. Various signs were placed on it, and it was dressed up for various occasions, such as a Santa Claus outfit at Christmas. The sign on the cutout that I liked the best was, "Give to the Rescue Mission." Sometimes I stand next to the cutout to see if students can tell which is the real me.

Pat and I were talking about the cutout, and I commented, "It looks better than I do." Her reply was, "It should look better. It's fifteen years younger."

Theft at the Biofeast

Before the cutout ended up at the bookstore, it had another adventure. At the end of each fall semester, I arranged for students and teaching assistants in my biology course to celebrate the end of the semester by having dinner at one of the large residential dining halls. There were hors d'oeuvres, nonalcoholic punch, tablecloths, decorations, a cake with my caricature on it, door prizes, and a special dinner. My cardboard cutout greeted people as they entered the dining hall with a sign, "Welcome to the Biofeast."

At the end of one Biofeast, I noticed that the cutout had disappeared. I described the situation to the class, and offered a $50 reward for information leading to its safe return, no questions asked. Anonymously, someone informed me that it had been seen on a student's personal Web site. It seemed unbelievable that someone would steal it and then put a photo on his Web site with his arm around it. I phoned the accused student and asked for the return of the cutout. It turned out that the student didn't know me and wasn't even in my class. Some other students had dropped off the cutout in his apartment the night before. He thought it was cute, so he had a photo taken with his arm around it.

26. Marvin standing next to his cardboard cutout in the Syracuse University Bookstore. Which one is the real Marvin? Photo by Steve Sartori.

I got it back the next morning, thinking that I had saved $50 since the tipster was anonymous. Then a teaching assistant found out who gave me the information about the cutout. I sent the student an email and asked her to drop into my office the next day about an important matter. The young lady showed up, looking apprehensive. I handed her an envelope containing a $50 bill and said, "Thank you." Case closed.

My Greatness

I have received many compliments over the years. Among other words, people have described me with such terms as "legendary," "hero," "cult," "a gem," "an institution," "warm and genial," "adorable," "charming," "inspirational," "sweet," "lovable," "svelte," "priceless," "awesome," "master test-question-writer," and "wild stallion." One student admired my clothing and asked, "Do you buy your clothes in Brooks Brothers?" I responded, "No, K-Mart."

Compliments went to my head and I became a living legend in my own mind. When I looked for a cap at graduation, I said to the director of graduation ceremonies, "I can't find a hat my size." She said, "No size is big enough to fit your head." I became convinced that I was truly great, and I talked about myself all the time.

My secret to success and fame was the "phantom payroll." Somehow I managed to find very capable people to do my work for me for free, and I took the credit.

Pat and I were having lunch in a local restaurant. An attractive lady at a nearby table smiled at me. Thinking of how famous I was supposed to be, I got up and walked to her table and said, "You look like you must know me." She replied, "No, but I'd like to," Pat hit me on the head with a manila envelope that she had in her hand.

Pat keeps my ego in check. She tries to remind me not to be a cheap, negative, self-obsessed grump who never wants to try anything new and always talks about myself.

We all know people who boast too much and keep telling everyone how great he or she is. Since nobody seemed to talk about my accomplishments, I began to wonder if I was so great after all. Here is the lesson I learned:

My Greatness

Nobody says I'm great,
So I have to tell them all
That I'm the greatest person
That anyone can recall.

Why do I boast so much?
Much more than someone should?
'Cause if I didn't praise myself,
No other person would.

But someone who is truly great
Has no need to say,
'Cause others do that job
In an enthusiastic way.

117

Humility

Being on campus for so long and being a cardboard cutout at the bookstore made me think I was famous. I was in an elevator with a professorial-looking man I didn't know. We chatted and he asked my name.

I said arrogantly, "I'm Marvin Druger."

"Oh, you're Pat's husband," he exclaimed. I immediately took a dislike to him.

A Long Day

We all have misadventures on airlines. One day, I was scheduled for a trip from Syracuse through Dulles Airport in Washington to Charlotte, North Carolina, to attend a two-hour meeting. I awoke at 4:45 A.M. to catch a 6:10 A.M. departure from the Syracuse Airport. I arrived about 5:50 A.M., only to be told that the plane had already boarded and that I should have checked in a full hour before the scheduled departure. An utterance of surprise and a few other unrepeatable comments earned me an exception. The airline agent gave me a boarding pass and told me to hurry. I went through security only to be told that my small cans of shaving cream, aftershave lotion, and so forth had to be put into a separate plastic bag to be screened. A security agent saw my distress and helped put the relevant items into the plastic bag.

I boarded the plane and was told that there was a maintenance problem. The plane sat on the ground, fully packed with people, for more than an hour. I asked the flight attendant if there was a toilet on board. "Yes," she replied, "but it's not working." After an uncomfortable flight, we arrived at Dulles Airport with barely enough time to get to the gate to catch the next flight to Charlotte. There I discovered that I had to board a bus shuttle to be transported to the proper terminal. I was driven across the airfield and I frantically raced to the departure gate.

I was too late. The plane had boarded and was closed to further boarding. The agent sent me to customer service, which was a good distance away. I sprinted to the customer service counter. There were ten people in line in front of me, and it seemed that I would certainly miss this flight also. Finally, I was given a boarding pass for another airline that would get me to Charlotte in time for my meeting. The gate attendant told me that I had to go through a security check again because I was switching from one airline to another.

"Where is the security area?" I asked.

"It's at the end of the corridor," she replied.

I looked down the endless corridor and thought to myself, "I'll never make it."

The agent noticed my concern and took pity on me. "Follow me!" she said, and she started running full-speed down the corridor. I took off after her. We ran a long way until we finally reached the security area of the new airline. My sweating face and heavy breathing must have attracted attention, because I was led into a caged area and body searched. Then the agent and I raced back to the gate, and I boarded the flight. I complimented the agent and myself on our excellent physical condition, as demonstrated by running so fast from the plane gate to the security area and back.

After we boarded the flight, the pilot told the passengers that there was a new time arrival system, and that plane would have to wait for departure. He announced, "When we leave, I'm going to fly this plane like I stole it to get us to Charlotte!" He received the message to depart, and he zoomed to Charlotte, but then we had to circle for about thirty minutes to wait for a landing time.

When we finally landed, I had to take an airport shuttle to take me to the main terminal to find transportation from the airport to the hotel. Amazingly, I did make the meeting. Incidentally, while walking on a conveyer belt at the Charlotte airport, I found a ten-dollar bill on the floor. I guess this was my lucky day!

Late Again

Pat drove me to the airport to catch a plane to a meeting in Chicago. We got off to a late start and there was a long line waiting to be checked in. I began to get anxious about whether or not I would make the flight. When I finally got to the counter, I was sweating from anxiety and I had that sick, sinking feeling in my stomach. "Do I still have time to make the plane?" I asked.

The agent replied, "You have plenty of time. Your flight isn't scheduled to leave until tomorrow." I had to call Pat to drive back to the airport to get me. She wasn't too happy about it. I had goofed again.

A Small Airplane

I had to make reservations to fly on a small commuter airplane. I said to the ticket agent, "I'd like a window seat." The agent replied, "On this plane, every seat is a window seat and an aisle seat." He was right.

The Missing Screw

When I fly in an airplane, I usually prefer a window seat, since I like to watch the wing to make sure that it doesn't fall off. On one plane, I noticed that there was a screw missing on the wing. I confirmed my observation with the passenger sitting next to me. When the plane landed, I told the pilot about the missing screw. He said, "Oh, we know about it. It's well within limits." I wondered what was beyond limits. Perhaps two screws missing?

Frightening Flights

We were in a jumbo jet flying from Sydney, Australia, to New York. There were three seats in a row, and I was sitting on the aisle, some stranger was sitting at the window, and Pat was sitting in the middle seat with our baby daughter on her lap. Suddenly, the plane encountered turbulence and dropped rapidly. The flight attendants who were serving coffee were thrown toward the ceiling. My baby's eyes popped open. I gripped the arms of the seat and thought, "This is it. It's a long way down." Instead of grabbing my arm for security, Pat grabbed the arm of the stranger at the window. She gripped his arm tightly until the plane bounced back to level flight. I never forgave her.

On another occasion, a flight from San Francisco hit severe weather as the plane neared Syracuse. I grabbed the arms of the seat and started sweating as the plane lurched up and down and side to side. I could see lightning. I was sure that we wouldn't make it this time. Fortunately, I was wrong. We made a safe landing. On my way out of the plane, I stopped at the cockpit and commented to the captain, "Tough landing."

He replied, "That was really something. Sometimes we have to work for a living."

I once interviewed a pilot on my *Druger's Zoo* program. I asked him if pilots were frightened when the plane was near a thunderstorm. "We're not frightened," he said. "We're prepared." That remark increased my confidence in pilots.

A Gas Puzzle

I drove into a gas station to get gas. I was alone in the car. I pulled up to the gas pump and realized that the opening to the car's gas tank was on the side of the car away from the pump. I thought that the gas pump hose might not be long enough to reach over the car to the gas tank opening. So I drove the car around the pump to the other side. Much to my dismay, the gas tank opening was still on the side away from the pump. I started to become panicky, and I drove around the pump three times trying to get the gas tank opening next to the gas pump. I finally figured it out, but it wasn't easy. And I have a Ph.D. Maybe that's why I couldn't figure it out.

The Sinking Ship

My son and I launched my motorboat at the public launching site at Owasco Lake and headed into open water toward my lake house dock. The boat had been serviced and stored for the winter, and it was in top condition. The bilge pump seemed overly active and soon water started accumulating in the boat. We frantically searched for the source of the leak, but we couldn't find it. Meanwhile, we had that sinking feeling. Finally, we reached my dock and hoisted the boat out of the water. I looked closely for the leak. Then, I noticed a small, round hole in the back of the boat. I called the owner of the marina. "The boat almost sunk. There's a hole in the back. Can you fix it?" He replied, "Sure. Just find the plug in the glove compartment and put it into the hole." That was easy. We avoided a Titanic disaster.

Bus Business

Pat and I were boarding a bus to take us from the Grand Canyon to a motel near Peach Springs, Arizona. Some large, rough-looking young men were guarding a few empty seats in the middle of the bus. As we attempted to sit in one of the seats, we heard, "These seats are taken." They reluctantly gave us one of the "saved" seats, but elderly people who boarded the bus had to move to the rear where the riding bumps were most pronounced on the rocky road. Each of the men was occupying a full double seat.

Pat complained to the bus driver. The driver's response was, "They're big men and they need room." Pat became furious and started yelling at the men for their lack of consideration. An angry exchange of words took place and, finally, one of the men said, "I'm older than you and deserve respect." Pat stretched her age a bit and responded, "I'm seventy years old."

Reluctantly, he replied, "Okay, so you're older. We'll move if you say 'please.'" I sat quietly awaiting the moment of truth. Many words passed through Pat's mind that are not printable, but she finally said, "Please." The men gave up their seats, and life moved on quietly. If they had physically attacked Pat, I was ready to defend her . . . I think.

Heron Island Cockroach

When we were in Australia, we visited Heron Island, a small tourist island on the Great Barrier Reef. Our cabin consisted of two narrow slabs with mattresses on them separated by a narrow aisle. There was a sink at one end of the aisle and a door on the other end. There was a light over the pillow of each bed.

One night, Pat suddenly cried out, "Yikes. There's something on my neck!"

I switched on the light and saw a giant cockroach on her neck. I said, "Hold still. I'll get it." I took a newspaper and folded it quickly. I was about to smash the cockroach when it flew away and disappeared into the sink area. Giant flying cockroaches are not my cup of tea. That night, I slept wrapped around Pat, in her narrow bed, with all the lights turned on. They were playing "Shake, Rattle, and Roll" on the loudspeaker, and that was when my oldest son was conceived. We owe him to a giant flying cockroach.

Hawaiian Cockroach

I rented a car in Hawaii. I was shocked when a cockroach ran across my arm while I was driving. I immediately returned the car to the rental agent. I told him about the cockroach. In the space on a paper that said, "Reason for Returns," he wrote, "Too much cockroaches." To me, one cockroach was too much.

Bomb?

We went on a tour of Israel and Egypt at a time when planes were being hijacked and hostages were being taken. A tour guide in Egypt gave me a manila envelope to deliver to the Israeli tour agency.

At the border, the Israeli security guard asked, "Did anyone give you anything to carry back to Israel?"

I remembered the envelope, and I said, "Yes, this envelope."

The guard jumped back. Then he looked in the envelope and saw that it was a bunch of brochures. He scolded me for bringing the package across the border into Israel. He said, "Do you know why we ask these questions?"

I said, "No."

He said, "Bomb!" Suddenly I understood his message.

Caves of Hercules

We visited the Caves of Hercules near Tangier, in Morocco. The guide spoke incoherently. At the end of the tour, he said one word clearly, "Tip."

The Chicken Farm

As a teenager, I worked on my uncle's chicken farm during the summer. It was exciting to have a chicken lay a warm egg in my hand. Rats that lived in the chicken coop often attacked chickens. One day, I decided to get rid of the rats. I tied a large spike to a broom handle and tried to spear the rats one by one. I was disappointed to discover that I was able to spear zero rats.

Vultures often cruised over the area. I wondered what a vulture looked like close up. So I lay on the roof of the chicken coop, pretending to be dead. I hoped that a vulture would come close enough so that I could study it in detail. Fortunately, the vultures were smarter than I thought. They never came near me.

Happy Thanksgiving

I was sitting at a table with a friend in a café in Chicago. A very attractive, well-dressed, middle-aged lady was buying some takeout food at the counter. After she paid for the items, she approached our table and handed me a five-dollar bill. "Have a happy Thanksgiving," she said. Before I could react, she said it again, "Have a very happy Thanksgiving" . . . and she walked out of the store. My friend and I were dumbfounded, and we couldn't figure out why she gave me that five-dollar bill. I was dressed in a jacket and tie and didn't look impoverished. Maybe, it was simply because I looked old? I could have given her a hundred-dollar bill from my wallet.

From then on, I have often thought about sitting in a cafe, looking sad, and hoping that someone will give me money. I haven't done it yet.

The Mailman

My daughter's dog hated the mailman. There seemed to be no good reason for this, but whenever the mailman approached the door, the dog went into a barking frenzy. Even seeing the mailman at a distance across the street set off this behavior. I suspect this reaction to the mailman was due to protective instincts of the dog. The dog knew that the mailman delivered mostly bills, and the dog tried to protect the family against financial loss.

Where's the Post Office?

Pat and I were driving around in Port Jervis, New York, looking for a post office. Pat finds directions only by using maps. I ask for directions from anyone who happens to be in the vicinity. We spotted a mailman. I opened the car window and yelled, "Do you know where the post office is?"

The mailman looked at me with a confused expression. "I don't have any idea," he said. I'm sure he was joking . . . or was he?

Property and Wealth

We had some money in stocks and mutual funds. Just before the stock market dropped, we were in good financial shape to buy property. One morning Pat announced, "I want to buy an apartment in New York City, so that we'll have a place to stay when we go there." We visit New York City very few times during the year, but I quietly agreed. We found a real estate agent and looked at apartments in Manhattan. We looked at a one-room apartment that was so high in the building that it was almost in the clouds. I wondered if there were oxygen masks in the closet. Despite the height, we could still hear the roar of traffic in the street below. The one-room apartment had a kitchenette and a tiny bathroom. Going up and down in the elevator was like going on a long-distance journey.

"How much?" Pat asked.

"Only $150,000," said the agent, "plus a few small monthly fees for parking and for the doorman."

That night, we were in bed at a hotel. I decided to compromise and say nothing. After a long period of silence, Pat said, "I don't think buying this apartment is a good idea." I breathed a sigh of relief.

Pat announced, "I want to buy a house in Maryland," where my daughter, son-in-law, and two grandchildren live.

"Why do you want a house there?" I asked.

"Because I want to live near a relative when I get old," she replied.

I said, "I'm a relative." Apparently, I was not the right kind of relative, so we ended up buying a town house near Cabin John Regional Park in Maryland. We rented the house to South American diplomats and we have been pleased about our purchase and rental. I'm certain neither of us will ever live there.

The house had a large family room on ground level and a large storage area that Pat really liked. "Plenty of room for storage," she remarked. A few months later, we visited the house to check on its condition. We were astonished to see that, without our permission, the tenant had built two bedrooms that now occupied two-thirds of the storage area.

Pat said, "But I liked the storage area."

I replied, "Don't worry. Now you can store stuff in the extra bedrooms."

The value of the house was increased, but we thought that even hanging pictures on the wall required permission of the owner. When the tenant moved out, he demanded $1,000 for constructing the bedrooms. Foolishly, we paid him.

My older sister was a widow living in a dilapidated apartment in Brooklyn, New York. There were termites, and the bedroom wall was on the verge of collapse. We decided to buy a house for her. She found one in Staten Island, New York. My sister lives there in a ground-floor apartment and her daughter's family lives upstairs. This purchase was our lifetime good deed.

Years later, Pat decided that we would buy a house on a lake. We drove all over the Finger Lakes in New York, but couldn't find anything that we really liked. Then on the way home, near Owasco Lake, I spotted a "For Sale" sign. "Hey, let's stop and look at this one."

Pat responded, "I'm tired. Forget it. Let's go home." Finally, I did convince her to look at the property. The owner allowed us to see the house even though there was no real estate agent present. There were large rooms, a wonderful complex of decks, a screened-in bug-free porch, and a paneled den. Our grandchildren were with us, and they wanted to know if the owner's cute little dog was for sale with the house. We loved the house even though all the walls were painted pink. We bought it, with no regrets ever, but we repainted the walls.

Occasionally, I think about my impoverished childhood in roach- and mouse-infested apartments. Somehow I went from extreme childhood poverty to senior wealth. Much of my financial success was due to skillful money management by Pat, and good luck.

For tax reasons, all the houses are in Pat's name. She is the property owner, so she gets all the mail and phone calls. As far as the outside world is concerned, I have ceased to exist. If we get divorced now, I'll be in deep trouble.

Kayaking

Pat and I grew fond of kayaking, especially since we had the kind of kayaks that don't overturn easily. My brother visited us at the lake, and I proudly showed him how simple it was to paddle. He tried it, and somehow the kayak capsized, and he fell into the water. "How did you enjoy kayaking?" I asked jokingly.

He replied, "It's great. It's just like swimming." And it was.

The Red Rental Car

I rented a red car on a trip. I stopped to get gas; Pat was alongside me in the front of the car. I went into the station to pay for the gas. I got back into the car, inserted the key in the ignition, and nothing happened. I repeatedly tried to turn the key to start the car. Then a huge man appeared at my open car window. "Going somewhere, buddy?" he asked in a threatening manner. I realized that I had gotten into the wrong red car. Pat was sitting in the rented red car at another gas pump thinking, "What the hell is he doing?"

The Blue Blazer

Pat and I went to a dinner party at a friend's house. I wore a blue blazer and a tie. Two days later, I was walking across campus wearing that same blazer and tie, I thought. I met a colleague who remarked, "Nice jacket."

"Yep," I replied, "it's an Edgeworth jacket," and I opened the jacket to display the Edgeworth label on the inside. The label was a Bill Blass label. I had mistakenly taken the wrong blazer when I was at the dinner party. It fit me better than my Edgeworth jacket, so I kept it.

Was It I?

I was at a meeting in a hotel. As I walked down a dimly lit hallway, someone jumped in front of me. "Excuse me," I said, and I tried to dodge the man. He jumped in front of me again. Then I realized that I was trying to dodge an image of myself in a wall-sized mirror. It would have been difficult for me to walk through me. This event prompted

the writing of a poem:

The Mirror Man

When I look into a mirror,
I see that I am there,
Every detail of myself
Is exceptionally clear.

The Mirror Man has features
That are the same as mine,
Our funny face and droopy nose
Are of the same design.

We look so much alike,
And he does all that I do,
I wonder if he thinks
The same thoughts I think too?

I tried to touch the Mirror Man,
But I hit against the glass,
The mirror blocked my way
And it would not let me pass.

So I just look in the mirror
And smile at what I see,
The Mirror Man is smiling too
'Cause he knows that he is me.

Wholesome Candy

Pat and I went to a movie with our family. Someone bought candy and passed it to each of us. I grabbed a piece and   133 put it into my mouth. "Boy, this candy is chewy," I said. That was because I didn't remove the wrapper and ate the candy, wrapper and all. It actually didn't taste too bad.

Soup and Salad

I arrived late to a business luncheon meeting. I apologized for being late and sat down at a table next to a woman at the luncheon. The waitress approached me: "Would you like a salad, sir?" she asked. "Yes, thank you," I replied. The waitress brought the salad. I took three large spoonfuls of salad dressing from the bowl near the woman, and spread the dressing on my salad. The woman next to me was horrified and exclaimed angrily, "That's my soup!" Now I know what's meant by soup and salad.

Names

My memory for names was never very good, especially as I grew older. I was talking to a married couple whose last name was Wolf. Another couple approached us. I introduced my friends: "I'd like you to meet Mr. and Mrs. Fox." Well, I guess they are both mammals, so this error was excusable.

Whenever I go to professional meetings where people are wearing nametags, I excuse myself for not remembering someone's name by saying, "I can't remember names, but I never forget a nametag."

I finally thought of a way to handle loss of memory for names. Whenever someone approaches me, whom I should know but whose name I can't recall, I say, "I'd like you to meet my wife, Pat." That's Pat's cue to say, "And what's your name?" Sometimes she forgets, and I have to repeat several times, "I'd like you to meet my wife, Pat," until she responds appropriately. In these cases, the person must think that I've developed a bad stutter.

Marketing and Sales

I wrote a book of poems for children of all ages, *Strange Creatures and Other Poems*. I sought a publisher, but was unsuccessful. "Who is your agent?" was the first question they asked. "What other children's books have you published?" was another question. Beneath the surface, there was the unspoken question, "How can a biology professor write a children's book? He's not one of us." So I published the book myself under the auspices of "Druger by the Lake Publisher."

More than 1,500 books were sold, and the distributor was the Syracuse University Bookstore, but I sold most of the books on my own. One lady made the mistake of asking me where the baggage claim area was at the airport. As we walked to the baggage claim area, I sold her a book. I sold a book to a waitress in a restaurant. I sold books to three naked men in the locker room at the health club. The price was $11.85, but they had no place to put the change. So I charged them $12.00. I sold a book to most people that I talked to on the phone. I put the price of the book on the cover of an exam for more

27. Bookmark to advertise Marvin's book *Strange Creatures and Other Poems*. The book costs $10.95 plus tax, and is available directly from Marvin (mdruger@syr.edu) or from the Syracuse University Bookstore (bookstor@syr.edu).

STRANGE CREATURES AND OTHER POEMS

MARV'S BOOK OF POEMS FOR CHILDREN OF ALL AGES

$10.95 plus tax/shipping/handling / For details contact **mdruger@syr.edu** / **315-443-9150** or Syracuse University Bookstore: on the web at **bookstore.syr.edu** or email at **bookstor@syr.edu** or telephone at **315-443-9901** / **Adventures in life for everyone** than 600 students. The last question on the exam was, "There is a fascinating book in the Syracuse University Bookstore entitled 'Strange Creatures and Other Poems.' What is the price of this book?" Nineteen students got the question wrong.

My one failure in selling a book was a man I approached in the locker room. "Got any grandchildren?" I asked.

"No," he replied.

"Got any children?"

"No."

"Got any nieces or nephews?"

"No," he said.

"Got any friends?" I asked.

"No," he replied.

"Forget it," I said, and I never told him about the book.

One dentist friend asked me, "How many books do I get for $100?"

"For $100, you can take them all," I replied. I was excited about the sale.

My ophthalmologist son placed a poetry book in each of the small waiting rooms in his office. A notice on the book said that they were available for purchase at the front desk. An acquaintance of mine said, "I just bought your poetry book at your son's office. I read it in the waiting room." He didn't mention that my poetry book was the only book in the room. A great way to increase sales.

Another big sale was to the former chancellor of Syracuse University. He was having lunch with his wife at the faculty club. I showed them a copy of the book. "I want ten copies," his wife announced. She didn't even want the faculty/staff discount, but immediately wrote a check for $118.50. I promised to deliver the books to the ex-chancellor in his office on the sixth floor of Bird Library. I went to the trunk of my car (which is my warehouse for the books, and anything else that Pat thinks she has thrown out). I gathered ten copies and added another as a free bonus.

I rushed to Bird Library and got on the elevator to the sixth floor. However, the elevator only went to the third floor. I was puzzled. Then, an attractive young lady ran out of her office and gave me a hug. It was a staff member who was a former student.

I asked, "What's going on? I must have taken the wrong elevator. How do I get to the sixth floor?"

She replied, "Well, if Mr. Newhouse had given us more money, we'd have a sixth floor." I was in the wrong building. I gave her the bonus copy of the book.

When I finally reached the ex-chancellor's office on the sixth floor of Bird Library, I asked, "To whom should I autograph the books?" The ex-chancellor gave me a list of five groups of grandchildren. I signed each book with the names in each group, but soon realized that I had several books left. He had expected me to sign each book to each individual grandchild. I had written several names in each book. "That's okay," he said, "Just sign two books to the same children. I'll give one to each." "Wow," I exclaimed, "That's why you're a chancellor."

28. Pat and Marvin reading *Strange Creatures and Other Poems.*
Photo by Steve Sartori.

The Curbs

Our street in Syracuse was once very wide. There were no curbs. Pat decided the street would look neater if we had curbs. She started a campaign and got neighbors to sign a petition to have curbs installed, and the city agreed to do the job. The street was resurveyed and became one-third narrower than it was before. All the neighbors found themselves with four feet of dirt between the old street boundary and the curb. The original street was wide because there had been extensive erosion over the years. The new curbs made the street as wide as it had been originally. I began to wonder if getting curbs installed was a good idea after all.

The day after curbs were installed on our street, I pulled into the driveway, accidentally drove over the curb, and split open the front tire. I bought a new one. The next year, I was making a sharp turn near the post office mailboxes and I hit the curb. Another split tire. A year later, on a snowy night, I was driving to my grandson's cello concert. I had to navigate a narrow space in the parking area. Guess what? Yes. I hit the curb and split open a tire. How many people do you know who split tires against a curb on three separate occasions? Curbs are not my thing.

Going Backwards

I've always had difficulty backing my car out of the driveway. No matter how I turn the steering wheel, I seem to trample grass or flowers at the sides of the driveway. At our lake house, we have one edge of the driveway lined with red guideposts, but even they don't help very much. One day, Pat was with me as I maneuvered backwards out of the driveway. As I scraped against a guidepost, she became alarmed. I said, "Don't worry. We'll get out." Her reply was, "In one piece, or two?" I have always admired Pat's sense of humor.

A Movie Star?

Some students approached me and asked if I would be willing to play a small but significant part in their student film. Of course, I agreed and I played the part of an old man. The movie was titled *Speed Date,* and I had two small roles to play. In one scene, I yelled out, "Love is a lie." This was the key line in the film. The film involved a couple that met at speed dating and got married. While they were consummating their marriage (with clothes on), the man proclaimed that they had to get divorced. She signed the divorce papers and he went back to the speed date hall to pick up another woman. So indeed, love is a lie.

I had no idea what the film was about, since I never saw a script. I simply played my brief role. At the end of the semester, the film was shown to a large audience of students and parents. Pat and I attended the film showing. A parent of the director of *Speed Date* saw me and enthusiastically said, "You were wonderful!"

When I saw the film in entirety, I felt embarrassed. Several of the scenes were risqué and politically incorrect. If the university chancellor had been there, I'm sure she would have thought, "I'll bet this was Marvin's idea." Anyhow, I liked the film and enjoyed playing my role as an old man. As time progresses, I seem to get better at this role.

Nincompoops and Bitter Herbs

Following my movie debut, students asked me to pay the part of an old man in two other student films. One was titled *Nincompoops*. Pat commented, "That fits you well."

The other film was *Bitter Herbs*. I had a long speaking part, and they had to hold the words in front of the listener's face while I read them. I couldn't remember any words, but my body language was superb. I'm now in between films, waiting for another invitation to play my typecast role of an old man.

Crime

All people have scary moments in their lives. One of mine was at a meeting in Puerto Rico. It was a warm night and I decided to walk from the Hilton hotel to my hotel on the other side of a bridge. A car pulled up to the sidewalk, and a man jumped out and stood in front of me in a crouched position. I didn't know what to do. I smiled and walked right past him. Then I realized that he probably wanted to rob me, and I ran away. I found a taxi and got back to the hotel safely.

A few weeks later, I met a woman who was also at the meeting in Puerto Rico. "Wasn't that you I saw that night running on the street?" she asked. She then told me that she was walking with a male companion. The same man who accosted me grabbed her purse from her shoulder and hit her friend on the head with a gun. The man had a gun that I never saw. Then I became frightened. A lucky escape from danger.

Pickpockets

I was on a crowded express bus in Los Angeles. I had to stand, and a young man carrying a plastic clothing bag stood next to me. We chatted a bit about sports. When the bus came to a stop, he walked toward the front of the bus to get off. I said, "Have a nice day."

He responded, "You're not going to have a nice day."

Instinctively, I felt for my wallet in my side pocket. It was gone. I then saw another young man getting off at the back door of the bus. I rushed to the exit and got off the bus. The two young men started running away, while I yelled to the crowd at the bus station, "Stop them. They stole my wallet!" Nobody responded.

I started running after the thieves. I was thinking, "These guys are drug addicts. I'm in good shape. I'll catch them." As I ran, I thought, "What do I do when I catch them? Punch them in the arm?" They ran down an alley. Wisely, I stopped chasing them and went into a pharmacy to phone the police. The line was busy.

Finally, the police arrived. I got into a police car, and the officer asked me questions and I started filling out forms. Another police car pulled up behind us. The officer next to me said, "Would you mind giving the information to the policeman in the car behind me? I'm off duty now."

I said, "I know what those guys look like. I want to see a police line-up."

The officer laughed. "We have people stabbed to death in this area, and there's no police line-up."

The policeman in the second car was kind enough to drive me close to my hotel. I got out of the car and had to walk about 100 feet to the hotel entrance. A coke bottle that someone threw out of a window crashed to the ground a few feet from me. I was supposed to return home in two days, but I left the next morning.

Actually, when I yelled at the thief when he got off the bus, he had dropped the wallet on the sidewalk. Someone picked it up, called Pat in Syracuse, and the wallet was returned to me. The only things missing were money and my AARP card. They missed getting a $50 bill that I had hidden in a secret pocket in my wallet. That was the part of my allowance that I use to buy Pat gifts.

House Burglary

I got up one snowy winter morning and went downstairs. I noticed that the window was open. I also noticed that the TV set was gone, along with Pat's pocketbook. I went out on the driveway to check for footprints. I suddenly realized that the car was also gone. I called the police. They looked at the footprints in the snow and announced, "Oh, it's the Johnson boys, David and Jesse. They've committed many robberies in this area. We can't arrest them unless we catch them in the act." The modus operandi of the Johnson boys was to take orders for TV sets and other items in advance. They would then shine a flashlight into houses to see if the items were there. Then, they would steal car keys and a car, deliver the goods to their customers, and drop the car off in the old Sears parking lot downtown.

Sure enough, the car was found in the old Sears parking lot, minus the TV set, Pat's pocketbook, and my coin collection. Since then, Pat never leaves her pocketbook downstairs, and I double-lock the doors.

The Garage Fire

My neighbor's canoe was wrapped in plastic and was leaning against the side wall of our garage. It was an extremely windy day, and an electric wire fell and hit the canoe. The canoe burst into flames, along with the side of our garage.

I was watching a ball game on TV near the window in the kitchen. "What's that sizzling noise?" Pat asked.

"Don't bother me now. I'm watching the game."

A neighbor called and said, "Your garage is on fire. I called 911." I guess I missed the fire because I was watching the game. I can't even remember who was playing or who won.

The firemen impressed me. They came immediately and calmly attacked the fire. One fireman seemed to enjoy smashing the side of the garage with an axe. While I watched in awe, a policeman pointed out a stranger standing in the driveway. "Do you know him? Is he a neighbor?"

"I've never seen him before," I replied. When the stranger saw us looking in his direction, he started running down the street. The police told me that criminals listen to police calls and show up at the scene of mishaps to see if they can steal something of value. That was a new twist that I had never heard about.

Watching TV

Television was a wonderful invention. With it, I could watch every sports event in existence. Pat dislikes watching sports on TV. Instead, she likes to watch hospital and doctors' programs. The more extreme the blood, gore, or disease, the better she likes the program. I said, "There's enough real-life disease. We don't have to watch it on TV also." My objections have had little effect on Pat's TV preferences.

With this discrepancy in our tastes for watching TV, the issue became who controls the remote control. One night, I went upstairs to the bedroom and discovered that Pat was asleep, with the TV showing some bloody surgery. I grabbed the remote control and changed the channel to watch the basketball game. "What are you doing?" came a ghostly wail. "I'm watching that program." I discovered that Pat could be asleep and still watch a program on TV.

Friends

Friends are hard to find, especially as we get older. We get suspicious of every new person we meet and suspect that they are somehow trying to defraud us. Friends can also be a nuisance because we have to work at friendships to maintain them. Although people think I'm friendly, I really would like to be left alone. Pat is much more sociable. Whenever she wants us to go somewhere, I say that I don't want to go. Then I compromise, and I go, and I usually have a good time. We even became members of a dance club that meets a few times a year for dinner and dancing. Although I was negative about this venture to begin with, I must admit that it was fun.

Whenever I go to a lunch or dinner meeting, I try to arrive early and sit at an empty table. I can tell who my friends are by seeing who sits at my table. I often end up sitting by myself. Pat is my best friend, and I like to keep it that way.

African Safari

Pat promised our granddaughter that, when she was fourteen, they would travel to Africa together. One day Pat saw a brochure about an Elderhostel Intergenerational Tour to South Africa. She could bring our fourteen-year-old granddaughter along.

Naturally, I said, "Forget it. I don't want to be attacked by terrorists or by wild animals or by bugs." I told Pat, "If I get malaria, I'll never forgive you."

Again, I compromised, and went to Africa. Of course, I had a wonderful, memorable time. It was winter in South Africa at that time, so there were no bugs. A South African reassured me: "If you see a mosquito this time of year, they're too weak to bite you."

Bargaining

Traveling around the world has enhanced my bargaining skills. Once I was shopping in a flea market in Bangkok. A woman was sitting on the ground making bathing shoes. I bargained with her and reduced the price of a pair of shoes from the equivalent of sixteen cents to eleven cents.

I was proud of my accomplishment until later that evening. I was ashamed of myself for taking advantage of this poor woman. I was so upset that I paid a young boy the equivalent of ten cents for a banana the next day. He was ecstatic.

The Carpet

We wanted to buy a carpet. Pat liked one in particular. "How much?" I asked.

"$6,000" was the store owner's reply.

"But I don't even like it. If I did, I'd pay that amount."

He immediately responded, "Okay. $4,000."

I whispered to Pat, "Can we afford $4,000?"

In a loud voice that the storeowner could hear clearly, she replied, "Sure, we can afford it."

"Be quiet," I said. "Let's go."

Pat looked dismayed. "I really like that rug."

"Well, I don't like it very much. Let's go." As we walked out of the store, I whispered to Pat, "Don't worry. He'll come after us."

As we reached the car door, a boy ran out to us. "Mister, my uncle wants to see you again." We bought the rug for $2,000. I'm sure the storeowner made his profit, and Pat learned to look the other way when I am bargaining for something.

A Granddaughter's Lesson in Bargaining

When we traveled to Africa with our fourteen-year-old granddaughter, her mother gave her $250 to spend for souvenirs. She wanted to buy an African mask. We were in a flea market, and she saw a mask she liked.

"How much?" I asked.

"$25."

"But I don't even like it. If I really liked it, I'd pay that price, but I don't really like it."

Our granddaughter gave me an angry look and said loudly, "My mother gave me $250 to spend, and she said I could buy whatever I wanted."

"Be quiet," I said. "Let's go." She sulked as we left the shop . . . only to return and buy the mask for $12. A lesson learned.

5 Getting Older

A common question is, "How did I get so old so fast?" The "golden years" come on very suddenly and, once they're here, most people don't think they are very golden. Some elderly people refer to these years as "the rusty years." Something is bound to go wrong with the body (or mind), and repairs are made by either chopping us open or stuffing us with pills. I was visiting my mother in a nursing home when the nurse wheeled in a cart with medicine bottles on it and announced, "Who takes pills?" Everyone raised a hand. It was like asking, "Who's still alive?"

Most of us don't really know what the pills do, but we take them anyhow. Somehow, we become convinced that the multivitamin pill and the baby aspirin will keep us alive forever. There is sheer panic whenever we miss taking a certain pill—if we remember that we missed taking it. I wrote a poem about pills:

Pills

Blue and yellow,
Pink and gray,

151

These are pills
I take each day.

When I was young,
I had no ills,
I had no need
For any pills.

Now that I'm old,
It's no surprise
That body parts fail
And illnesses arise.

Pills are now my friends,
They comfort me each day,
They keep my juices flowing
And chase the pains away.

I used to take just two a day,
I now take more than five,
Pills, pills, and more pills
Now keep me alive.

I met an eighty-five-year-old former professor who retired about twenty-five years ago. When I first recognized him, I was going to say, "John, I thought you were dead." I didn't say it, but I asked him about his health. He said, "My doctor says I'm in great shape. He said that my cholesterol level is perfectly normal. What's perfectly normal at my age is to be dead." I didn't respond.

Senior Discounts

One of the great rewards of old age is the senior discount. They should give the discount to the younger people who can't afford to pay. I can afford it, but I always ask for the senior discount anyhow. There is great satisfaction in saving 35 cents. As a senior, I can eat lunch at McDonald's for less than $3.00 . . . a hamburger, a small fries, and a senior drink. Sometimes, fast food restaurants only offer medium and large fries. The medium fries look strangely similar to the outdated small fries. Sometimes the senior drink is a half-sized cup . . . but I'm told that refills are free. Sometimes they give you a regular-sized cup. Again, there is that sense of senior satisfaction.

Pat looks very young. I was negotiating my senior discount at a movie. The ticket agent looked at Pat and said, "I'm not giving *her* a discount." That remark to Pat made me feel even older.

Another time, I went to the movies with Pat and I forgot to ask for the discount. After getting the ticket, I went back to the ticket agent. "I forgot to ask for my senior discount." He replied, "I already gave it to you." From then on, I wanted storekeepers to "proof me" for my age. Nobody has.

Once I asked for a senior discount at McDonald's and the worker remarked, "You can't possibly be old enough to be a senior." I was so pleased at that remark that I paid the full price.

Social Security

Another blessing of old age is social security. After you reach the age of eligibility, you can receive social security payments, even if you are working full time. When I approached my sixty-fifth birthday, and became eligible to collect social security, I was told that I'd get more money per month if I waited until later to start receiving payments. I thought, "This *is* later." I started collecting social security at age sixty-five.

Life Cycles

Life offers a series of cycles. We start young and then age, and then we start again. For example, we start high school as freshmen and become seniors. Then, we start college as freshmen and become seniors. Then we start jobs as freshmen and become seniors. Eventually, we become the ultimate seniors. In life, we have many opportunities to make the transition from freshman to senior, and we acquire knowledge and wisdom through these cycles. We finally know about life, but passing on this senior wisdom is problematic. The younger freshmen always think they have a better way of doing things. But do they?

The payment cycle is another interesting feature of growing older. As a freshman, we are eager to establish a reputation. When we are asked to do something special, we do it for free. As we progress in life, we start getting paid for special activities. That's nice, and we will do some things for pay and some free. Then we get to a stage where we only do a special job if we get paid for doing it. As we approach older age, we start doing some things for free once again. Finally, when we are older, we volunteer and do everything for free, because we are so glad someone asks us to do it.

I have been doing poetry readings at elementary schools. My largest payment for this activity was an unsolicited $15 gift certificate for Dunkin Donuts. I discovered that I could get a lot of donuts for $15, but my real payment has been the enthusiastic responses of the children.

Retirement

You know you've gotten older when people start calling you "sir." I told my colleague at Syracuse University that I would quit teaching and retire as soon as my students started calling me "sir." He replied, "I just met five students who called you sir." I know what he was thinking.

Retirement is a major life change. They say that you know when it's time to retire. That's true. You become more sensitive and irritable, and every comment from a colleague is perceived as an insult. They leave you out of things that you think that you should be involved in. The many contributions that you made during your years of employment are quickly forgotten. It took many years to gain wisdom, and now that you finally know how to deal with the issues, nobody wants to listen. "Out with the old, in with the new" is the theme.

People who retire because there's something they want to do that their job prevented them from doing adjust well to retirement. People who retire just because they reach a certain age have difficulties coping. When Pat retired from working as an administrator at Syracuse University, she didn't know what to do with herself. For several weeks, she slept late and just hung around. Then she found volunteer interests. She became a docent at the Erie Canal Museum; she became involved in several clubs, a book discussion club and the Syracuse University Women's Club; she took up mah-jongg, knitting, quilting, and sewing; she got some part-time secretarial work; she volunteered to do tax returns for AARP; and she became a member of the Friends of Jowonio Board. She has so many interests that I hardly see her any more. When we do see each other, we appreciate each other more. This is another way to have a long, happy marriage.

I met a friend whom I hadn't seen for awhile. He asked, "How's Pat?" Referring to how busy she was, I jokingly replied, "Who's Pat?" He said with surprise, "Are you still together?" Welcome to the modern world.

Retirement Advice

Syracuse University offered different deals for older individuals who wanted to retire. Since I was getting closer to that stage of life, I wanted to find out what these deals were. I didn't want to ask the dean or chairs, since I would then be labeled as a potential retiree. So I checked the university phone book and found a listing for the "Faculty and Staff Assistance Program." I called the director of the program and told her what information I was seeking. She said, "I may be able to help you. Why don't we meet privately somewhere?" I went home and told Pat about this romantic request. It turned out that the unit I contacted was the psychiatric help unit on campus. I cancelled the appointment and told the director that I didn't think I needed that kind of help now, but that I might well need it in the future.

Aging and Sex

Sex is at the core of relationships, but friendship is far more important. Pat is my best friend. She is always there in time of need, but most important, we share the adventures of life together and have plenty of laughs.

Many say that sex diminishes with age. There are indeed changes that occur. We sleep together in a king-sized bed. In our early married days, we slept in a regular-sized bed with my body wrapped around her. After fifty years of marriage, she sleeps on one edge of the bed and I sleep on the other edge. The only thing wrapped around her is the blanket. Pat has become a fidgety sleeper, and she often ends up sleeping on the floor, or she sleeps in another bedroom.

One day, after fifty years of marriage, I got a fancy hotel room in Washington, D.C., while I was attending a meeting. My daughter lives near D.C. and Pat slept at her house. I slept alone in the hotel. Next time I travel with Pat, I think I'll reserve a hotel room for only one person. But despite momentary separations, our passion for each other still persists after all these years. How nice.

Infirmities of Older People

Old age invariably brings infirmities. The ligaments that I tore playing basketball in my youth suddenly start hurting. The great posture that I exhibited as company commander in the Coast Guard Reserve has turned into sagging shoulders. I have to blink a few times, or use my magnifier to read names in the phone book. They have made the print much smaller in the newspaper. Life takes on a blurred appearance.

I had my eyes checked by my ophthalmologist son. I'm far-sighted in one eye and near-sighted in the other. Both eyes together work pretty well, but I probably could see better with glasses. I refuse to get glasses. They slip off your nose, you lose them, you sit on them, you forget where they are. The optometrist said, "Okay. No glasses, but just don't get dirt in one eye when you're driving."

I never was very good at remembering names. Now I can hardly remember any names. Sometimes I have to think for a while to recall that my wife's name is Pat. Whenever I get worried about memory loss, I remind myself of a doctor's comment: "If you know you're forgetting, you're okay. If you don't know that you're forgetting, then you're in trouble."

Older people also tend to repeat themselves. After I said the same thing three times, Pat once asked, "Don't you get tired of repeating yourself?"

I said, "That's because you don't listen the first time."

"How about the hundredth time?" she replied.

Socialization

Older people like to talk and socialize. Nursing homes often have amateur entertainers do performances for the residents. They are generally terrible, but the older people love their performances. The topic of conversation among older people often centers on questions such as Who died recently? Who has which disease? And what did the doctor say about my latest ailment? The saddest thing to see in nursing homes is older people with sharp minds but withered bodies. There are people who are confident that they can do it, but they really can't. Aging does take its toll.

Instant Aging

I recall the moment when I went from being a young man to an old one. When I was in my twenties, I was hiking in the woods and came to a small stream, about eight feet wide. There was a rock in the middle, and I thought that I would jump and land one foot on the rock and leap across the stream. As I jumped, I had the thought, "I could fall and get hurt." I fell into the water. The realization that I was not superhuman hit hard. Youth thinks it is invincible until reality proves otherwise. I went from being a young man to an old one in that instant. I don't try to jump across streams anymore.

Exercise and Diet

Exercise and diet are supposed to be good for us at any age. I exercise regularly. Jogging and Nautilus weight lifting are two of my activities. I have been lifting the same weights for many years, but it doesn't get any easier. At one time, I played basketball for the old man's basketball team at the university, that is, the Geriatrics. Usually, the coach would put me in the game for the last few minutes. At the first sight of sweating, he would take me out for fear that I'd have a heart attack. When we played the champions of the student league, they slaughtered us. Instead of demanding more playing time, all the Geriatrics begged to be taken out of the game.

The university was involved in a national running competition. We would be timed and points would be given for our performance. I had a lucky day and ran a mile at a good pace. The timer stood at the end of the mile and clocked us. I ended up with a 6:01 mile. If the timer had given me some indication that I was so close to six minutes, I might have surged ahead and broken the six-minute mile. I never did. Nowadays, I'm pleased to be jogging at any speed.

I boasted to a colleague about my 6:01 mile. She said to another colleague, "Did you know that Marv did a 6:01?" He replied, "What distance?" Another ex-friend remarked, "You did a 6:01. That's great. How long did it take you?"

I jog regularly around an indoor track at the health club. The track circles a central area that has weights and exercise machines. Most of the track is blocked from view by a wall. There is a length of the track about twenty yards that is visible to the machine exercisers and weight lifters.

I met a young lady who was a real runner. Michelle is built like a feather and she flies around the track at tremendous speeds. While I plod around the track, she races past me. I can feel the breeze as she passes by.

I thought of a great idea to increase my prestige as a runner. I would wait at the edge of the open track area and would run with Michelle for the twenty open yards and then slow down to my usual snail's pace. Then I would run the twenty yards with her when she appeared again three laps later. Nobody seemed to notice that I was missing for several laps. A club member asked, "Who's Marv?" Someone replied, "Oh, he's the guy that runs with Michelle." I fooled everyone and became respected as a real runner.

After one of my fake runs, I asked a friend who was lifting weights, "Did you see me zoom around the track with Michelle?" He replied, "No." I was disappointed that my energy had been wasted.

After a recent jog around the track, Pat asked me, "Why are you staggering around the track?" I replied, "I wasn't staggering. That's the way I run."

I was jogging on a road and my daughter who was walking her dog in the opposite direction approached me. When she got close enough to recognize me, she said, "Dad. I thought you were running?" I *was* running.

161

A neighbor near our Owasco Lake house remarked, "I've seen you walking by our house many times." I *never* walked by his house. I always *ran* by his house. At least, I thought I was running.

Aging does slow us down physically. I first noticed this one day while I was jogging in the street. I observed that the trees and houses were passing by much more slowly than before. I tried to increase my pace, but the trees and houses didn't seem to care. They still passed by more slowly than before.

My exercise routines made me believe that exercise is not really very important for good health. It's the shower that does the trick. If you pretend to exercise and take a shower, you feel just as good. So why bother torturing yourself with the exercise?

I have a friend who hates to exercise. Every time he gets the urge, he lies down until it goes away. He also believes that we are born with a fixed number of heart-beats, and if we exercise, we use them up faster.

Whenever a person at the health club is being given a tour of the facilities, I always interrupt and say, "If you join, you start looking like me." This remark may have discouraged many people from joining the club.

The Fatal Hot Dog

My daughter was a dietitian in a nursing home. She told me about an eighty-six-year-old lady who wanted to eat a hot dog. The lady had high blood pressure and was on a low-salt diet. The doctor refused to let her have hot dogs. I think that she should be allowed to eat that hot dog. Personally, I like them. Whenever I eat one, I ask myself, "Will this kill me?" Who do you know who has been killed by eating one hot dog? When you reach a certain age, you should be allowed to eat anything that you want to eat . . . if you still have teeth to chew the food.

The House

We bought our Syracuse home from an old widower in 1965. Almost fifty years later, I was at the health club and an old man came up to me and asked, "Aren't you the person who bought my house on Ramsey Avenue?" I was shocked. How could he still be alive? He was probably 120 years old. It turned out to be his son who was now quite old. Time does pass quickly.

The Wildcat Reunion

Several years ago, we received a postcard inviting Pat and me to attend the reunion of my childhood gang. Following my pattern of negative behavior, I said, "No. I want to forget those guys and those days of poverty."

Pat said, "But they were my friends, too." So we compromised and attended the reunion in a restaurant in Greenwich Village, in New York City. Everyone had the same personality, even though there were some physical changes. We had a wonderful time.

One Wildcat said, "The only good thing about getting old is the senior discount." Another member responded, "I'd rather pay the full price."

I talked about the possibility of training for a triathlon. Jokingly, I said that the training should involve "eating, sleeping, and sex." My friend responded, "Great idea, but thirty years ago, the order would have been reversed."

Then BZ, the leader of the Wildcats said, "Okay, let's stop talking about the past. Let's talk only about the future. What nursing home do you want to go to? And do you want to be buried or burned?"

Now the Wildcats get together once each year. One year, we inhabited the Paris Hotel in Las Vegas. Another year, we took a cruise ship to Nova Scotia. Another year, we attended the wedding of BZ's son. The number of Wildcats have thinned with time, but the survivors stayed vibrant, active, and friendly. Old friendships don't fade away. Despite the tragedies of life that strike everyone sooner or later, the bonds among us stayed strong. We never really grew old.

Telling and Listening

Telling and listening are both part of human interactions. Most people prefer telling and are not very good listeners. They wait politely or impatiently to tell their story. "I had a bad cold last week." "*You* had a bad cold, you should hear about the cold that *I* had." People also like to talk about themselves, and "I . . . I . . . I . . . me . . . me . . . me . . ." are frequent parts of conversations. Yet everyone loves a listener. I realize the importance of listening, and I'm trying to concentrate on not talking so much, especially about myself, and listening to what the other person has to say.

I rarely listen to what Pat says. At the breakfast table, Pat will tell me something. A few seconds later, I would ask her about that topic. She refuses to repeat herself, so I remain uninformed about what she said. I'm trying to concentrate on paying attention.

One day, Pat asked me to buy one new calendar to hang over a stain on a wall in our house. As we were driving to the store, I asked, "How many calendars do you want me to buy?"

"How about thirty-five?" she replied. "Then I can wallpaper the wall with them." I bought only one calendar.

I recall telling Pat about childhood experiences. I told her how Mrs. Davidson, my teacher in elementary school, used to grab me by the chin and shake it. "That's why my jaw looks that way." Pat's response was, "How do you explain your nose?" I told a friend about Pat's comment and he asked, "How *do* you explain your nose?"

Older people are often talkers and not listeners. They talk about their diseases and who died most recently. It is almost a competition over who's suffering the most. Older people also talk about the good old days. My mother-in-law claimed that Elvis Presley was the beginning of the end of the world. Older people always claim that things were better in the old days. Maybe they really were.

6 Health Happenings

The human body is remarkable. Despite the tremendous complexity of parts and functions, the body works well most of the time. When it doesn't work well, there are many procedures and drugs to restore health. Pat and I have had our share of deviations from normal body functioning. Here are some of the health hazards we have encountered in our lifetime.

Pyloric Stenosis

When our oldest son was born, Pat breastfed him. After about four weeks, my son started to regurgitate the breast milk and the milk would forcibly shoot out from his mouth. The doctor detected a small nodule on his abdomen. The nodule was an enlargement of the pyloric muscle that regulates the passage of food from the stomach to the small intestine. Eventually, the muscle enlarges enough to block the passage of food, leading to complications. Fortunately, there is a surgical procedure that involves slitting the muscle so that food can pass. Normal functioning returns and the patient can live happily ever after.

There is evidence that pyloric stenosis is more common in firstborn sons and that it has a hereditary basis. When I first learned about the condition, I scolded Pat: "I never should have married you. There are all these 'bad' genes in your family." Then, I discovered that one of my cousins had the condition, and the "bad" genes were in *my* family. She never should have married me.

Pat's Aching Back

Pat's back started to hurt. A few days later, the pain became so intense that she could not walk down the stairs in our house. So I called 911, and an ambulance came to take her to the emergency room. I was very tired, and I thoughtlessly left her lying in agony on a bed in the emergency room. I went home to go to sleep.

A few hours later, I received a phone call from the emergency room asking me to take Pat home. Pat often reminds me of this lack of consideration and my poor judgment. The lesson learned is to prioritize your values, and recognize that family comes first.

The wife of a prominent scientist developed terminal cancer. The scientist immediately retired and spent several years at the bedside of his wife, until she died. I have always admired him for that decision. That's what love is all about.

Hospital Wait

That was not the first time I had been unintentionally inconsiderate about Pat. She had had a dilatation and curettage (D and C) and had been released from the hospital. She called me and told me to pick her up immediately. I said, "I'll be right there." Then I got a phone call and forgot about picking her up. She stood waiting outside the hospital for more than thirty minutes. When I finally arrived, she was near collapse. I guess that phone call wasn't that important after all. I needed to get my priorities and values straight.

The Expensive Pill

We were in California, expecting to leave the next day on a plane to Syracuse. Pat had a bad sinus infection. A hotel house doctor examined her and prescribed some pills.

I rushed to the pharmacy with the prescription. "How much are the pills?" I asked.

He replied, "$18 each."

Without considering Pat's health, I asked, "Do you have anything cheaper?"

I bought the pills, however. I gave them to Pat and said, "Let the pill dissolve in your mouth. It may last longer than swallowing it." We did get home safely the next day, and Pat's sinus infection seemed a bit better. Maybe it's best not to swallow pills after all.

Locked Out

It was a cold and snowy day. Pat had just been released from the hospital where she'd been treated for a back infection. She had a cane and could barely walk. I accompanied her into a store to buy a device for her back. When we left the store, I thoughtfully announced, "Pat, you wait here and I'll drive the car to the front of the store so that you won't have to walk." I ran to the car and drove up to the front of the store. I got out of the car to help Pat. When we returned to the car, I discovered that I had locked the door with the engine running and the key inside. Pat went back into the store to wait while I called my son, who had a key to my car. He arrived just before the gas was gone and saved the day.

The Brace

The doctors were measuring Pat's body to fit her for a back brace. One doctor remarked, "She's not chesty, but she's broad."

The other doctor said, "Yes. She's medium in front and large in the back." Just the words a woman likes to hear.

Back-Biting

I was a discussant at a symposium where dental researchers presented their research. During the discussion period, one researcher said that Vionella (the bacterium that infected Pat's back) "was common in the human mouth and it was harmless."

I raised my hand and asked, "Then how come it gave my wife a back infection?"

He responded, "What did you do, bite her on the back?" After all the issues with Pat's back infection, it was me who needed the morphine.

Pain

Pat had a Caesarean operation when our daughter was born. She had two more Caesarean operations for our other two children. Two weeks after the third operation, Pat was lying in bed, and I was standing next to her, showing her a book that I had bought. "It's amazing," she exclaimed, "I feel absolutely no pain." Then I accidentally dropped the book on her abdomen. She felt pain after all.

The Colon

Many of my former students are successful physicians. When I had a twisted colon, I had to go to the emergency room at the hospital. The attending doctor was a former student of mine. He examined me and said, "You may be impacted." As he put on rubber gloves to do a rectal exam, he commented, "I guess it's payback time."

Hospitals Can Be Fun

When part of my colon was surgically removed because of some twists, everything went wrong, and I spent a month in the hospital. I had fever and chills, hiccoughs every five seconds for fourteen days, allergic reactions to medicines, and a large abscess that pressed on my diaphragm. But I had great care. All the nurses were my former students, and so were some of the doctors. Everyone visited me to cheer me up. My only real concern was when the Baptist minister, the rabbi, the Protestant chaplain, and the Catholic priest visited me. "Why were they there?" I wondered.

Starvation in the Hospital

At mealtimes, a hospital aide delivered my meal in a tray with a heavy cover on it, and set the tray down on a table about six feet away from me. Pat was often there to help me at mealtimes. When she was not there, I rang for the nurse to help me reach the food. Frequently, the nurse didn't come. About thirty minutes later, the food delivery person took away the tray with the food uneaten. After a week of this scenario, the nutritionist visited me. "You seem to be losing weight," she said, "You should eat more."

The Handshake

The last week that I was in the hospital, a young resident attended to my wounds. He dressed the wound daily and comforted me. The last day of my hospital stay, he grabbed my hand and gave me a warm handshake. "I just want to thank you for all you did for me," he said. I couldn't imagine what I had possibly done. He explained that he had intended to be a geology major, but took my biology course. He came into my office to discuss his future. I apparently encouraged him to become premed. He went on to study medicine and he loved it. I had tears in my eyes when the man in the bed on the other side of the curtain in my room exclaimed, "And my daughter-in-law took your course also."

Seizures

At age sixty-four, I started having seizures. An MRI revealed a tiny cyst on my brain that might be the cause. I started taking antiseizure medication. The level of medication in the blood had to be checked regularly, as the effective level should be between 10 and 20 units. One day, I was crossing the street to get to the university parking lot. Suddenly, I wasn't there anymore. The next thing I knew, someone was hovering over me as I lay on the ground. "Who is the president of the U.S.? What's your phone number?"

I was rushed to the emergency room, and they discovered that the level of medication in my blood had dropped to 3 units. The outcome of this experience was positive. I realized that dying was not so bad. The curtain drops and that's it. Of course, those who you leave behind are distressed. In this instance, consciousness returned, and I did remember the president's name and my phone number.

Aunt Tess and Alzheimer's Disease

Pat's aunt Tess developed Alzheimer's disease. This disease of the brain progresses over time. Memory loss is one of the key symptoms. I visited Aunt Tess one day when she was in my mother-in-law's apartment. When I entered the room, Aunt Tess exclaimed, "Handsome!" Actually, I think she was not mentally ill at all.

Prostate Surgery

When you get older, most of the friends you have are either retired, terminally ill, or dead. If they live long enough, many men develop prostate problems. A nurse practitioner felt a hard spot on my prostate, and they decided to do a biopsy. While the doctor was doing the procedure, I told him jokes and he laughed. I said, "I shouldn't be telling jokes while you're doing this." He replied, "This is not the first biopsy I've done."

In the old days, after diagnosing prostate cancer the doctor would simply tell you what to do. Nowadays, the doctor tells you the options, and you have to decide. "Leave it alone, and it may start bothering you in fifteen years." In fifteen years, I'd likely be dead from something else, but I didn't like the thought of having cancer.

I checked with a radiologist, and he recommended surgery. The surgery went well, but the aftereffects were not pleasant. I was told, "You've lived with that organ for more than seventy years, so it's like losing a friend. It's difficult to get used to being without it." I would tell friends, "I feel great from the waist up and from the thighs down. My middle needs some work." Since the operation, I've met many men who have had a similar experience. The prostate is in a complicated part of the body. Someone asked, "How come men have the sewage system and the entertainment center in the same place?" I have no answer.

While I was suffering from the aftereffects of my operation, people would ask, "How do you feel?" I usually responded, "Okay." Pat said that I was being too negative. Thereafter, when people asked me how I felt, I said, "Pat says that I'm feeling great!"

A Missing Person

I had the prostate surgery in Northwestern Hospital in Chicago. After I was discharged, Pat and my son met me in the lobby. Pat said, "I'll go upstairs to get the medicine you need. Wait here for me." It took some time and I was restless. I said to my son, "James, you wait here for Mom. I don't feel so good, and I'm going to the hotel." I left the hospital to walk back to the hotel, which was about two blocks away. I got lost on the streets of Chicago and had

no idea where the hotel was. I didn't feel well, and had no

identification and no money. After about an hour, however, I miraculously found the hotel. I went to the room, but my son and Pat were not there. "I guess they went shopping," I thought, and I lay down on the bed to rest.

About an hour later, the phone rang. It was Pat. She was frantic about my absence and had called the police. I had been listed as a missing person. While the police searched for me, my son drove his scooter up and down the streets looking for me. They were sure I was in a morgue somewhere. Finally, Pat and my son got to the hotel room, and Pat called the police to cancel the search. Pat explained what had happened.

The officer on the phone said, "Is he okay now?"

Pat replied, "He's okay now, but I'm going to murder him!" I wondered if this threat could have resulted in some sort of prison term. My son learned a lesson, and so did I.

The Mysterious Anesthesia

When my colon became twisted, it required emergency surgery. I was screaming as two doctors held my arms while a third doctor held a needle to inject my back with something. He said, "I'm going to give you an epidural. We give that to pregnant women." I started to laugh and, suddenly, I was lying in bed with a doctor about a foot from my face saying, "It's over. The surgery went well."

This experience made me very suspicious about anesthesia. It suddenly occurred to me that I could be anesthetized and never wake up. I could actually die.

Years later, when I had my prostate removed, I was especially alert about anesthesia. I was in my hospital room when a doctor walked in and said, "Hello. I'm the anesthesiologist." I said hello, but was careful not to shake his hand.

A few minutes later, another doctor entered the room. "Hello, I'm the assistant anesthesiologist." Again, I was careful not to shake her hand or let either of them come near me.

Then I awoke, and a doctor was a foot from my face saying, "It's over. The surgery went well." This was a mystery. Neither anesthesiologist ever came near me, yet somehow I had been anesthetized. This convinced me that modern medicine has made many advances.

Lowering Blood Pressure

High blood pressure is common among older people. They say that exercise and diet can lower blood pressure. Another effective way to lower blood pressure is to have organs removed through surgery. After I had part of my colon removed and, years later, the prostate, my blood pressure dropped to normal. Try it and see.

7 Lessons in Life

After more than seventy-five years of living, I'd like to offer some observations about life, derived from the many misadventures described in this book.

1. The years go by very quickly. It seems like yesterday that I was forty years old and worried about the midlife crisis that came at that time. Apparently, insignificant events become imbedded in your memory, and often come to mind when you least expect it.

Hundreds of miscellaneous thoughts could easily be brought to mind, especially when you have reached your mid-seventies. We are the product of all of our experiences, and we don't know which ones will be rooted in our unconscious in detail, waiting to emerge at odd moments.

2. There's no such thing as a bad experience. We learn from everything that we do, and everything that we do becomes part of what we are. My strong emphasis on class attendance reflects this theme. We are the culmination of all the experiences we have ever had. So, we should seek experiences that are likely to enrich our lives.

3. Every individual is unique and has special talents. Someone can be taller, richer, and smarter, but nobody is *better* than anyone else. We should try to identify our unique talents and nurture them. We should also recognize, appreciate and respect the unique talents of others. The barber who cuts my hair sings at a well-known restaurant and hosts a radio program on Sunday mornings. A chemistry professor is the conductor of a brass band. A physics professor plays bongo drums in a band. They aren't supposed to be able to do these things. Why not? Each of us has unique talents and we need to try to discover them. Many of my misadventures in this book are unique; others are episodes that can and do happen to many people. Have you ever driven around the gas pump to get the gas tank opening on the same side as the pump?

4. Luck plays a big role in life. I was lucky to be lucky. The result of my good luck was my wife, three children and seven grandchildren, and a professional life that helped others shape their lives. The good fortune is to find where your unique talents fit in life. Without thinking much about it, my life happened, and I ended up where I think I fit.

People can increase their chances of being lucky, if you place yourself in situations where good things are more likely to happen. If I hadn't gone to the high school sorority party when I was twenty years old, I would never had been lucky enough to meet Pat.

5. Health happens. As we get older, we are bound to get some health problem that we don't want. The longer

we live, the more likely this will happen. We try to survive as long as we can, but the reality of life and death become more apparent as we age. We can eat a proper diet, exercise regularly, have a healthy lifestyle, do everything right, but we still will die. My friend says he looks forward to getting older, considering the alternative. We don't know why every living thing eventually dies, but it happens, and we need to be psychologically prepared.

How we prepare for death is a very personal thing. We live interacting with others, but we die alone. I think it's important to be aware of the inevitability of death, and recognize that we are no different from countless other living creatures in this regard. The natural climax to all life is death. When we die, the lights simply go out. The sad part of death is not the one who has died, but loved ones who are left behind. Psychological preparation for death involves developing a realistic view of the nature of life.

6. Relationships are important. Everyone has to relate to others to survive, but many people never have a close relationship with another individual. They may have many associates, but no true friend. Although I have talked about Pat in a humorous context, she is my true friend and we have shared the misadventures of life together. Despite my joking about Pat in this book, she is beautiful, intelligent, knowledgeable, dependable, caring and talented. She not only has my love and friendship, she also has my deepest respect as a human being. I was very fortunate that, when she was fifteen, she couldn't find the

right key to her apartment door, and that the elevator was not on the fifth floor.

7. Have fun in life. Don't take everything too seriously. Those individuals who see humor in life are best able to live it fully. There is a humorous side to every tragedy. We have the capacity to laugh, so laugh a lot . . . It's good for you!

The End

This book was written on three different computers. After the book was completed, I couldn't identify which

29. Pat and Marvin hugging each other as they move on in life
together. Photo by Steve Sartori.

manuscript on the different computers was the final one. I had the material stored under such headings as: "total final composite," "revised composite," "ultimate final copy," and "ultimate last copy." I had to ask the publisher to send me a copy of the manuscript, so that I could make revisions. What you have read is the "ultimate, ultimate, definite final copy." I hope that you have enjoyed reading the book, and that my misadventures have made you think, laugh, and appreciate life more fully. Changing behavior, based upon self-reflection, is very difficult, but I hope this book has helped you do just that.

We are each the product of our experiences, and we remember life's episodes that are imprinted as memories in our brain. **Marvin Druger** has lived more than seventy-five years, has a wife, three children, and seven grandchildren, and many memories. Marvin told a friend that this book would contain all the stupid things that he has done in his life that people could relate to and laugh at. His wife, Pat, commented, "And it will be a very fat book."

Marvin is now a professor emeritus in biology and science education after fifty-five years of teaching science, mainly the introductory college biology course at Syracuse University. He was president of three international science education organizations: the National Science Teachers Association, the Society for College Science Teachers (twice), and the Association for the Education of Teachers in Science (now known as the Association for Science Teacher Education). He has contributed in countless ways to science education, and this book reveals his talent for writing in other areas. He spends his spare time reading, writing, exercising, doing a radio program *(Science on the Radio)*, directing a Saturday science enrichment program for high school students, presenting readings of his poetry book *(Strange Creatures and Other Poems)*, enjoying the company of Pat and his family, and laughing at himself. He has a house on Owasco Lake in Auburn, New York, where he can think, write, and relax.